RUGBY LEAGUE LIONS
AN ILLUSTRATED HISTORY OF THE GREAT BRITAIN RUGBY LEAGUE TEAM 1907–2001

LES HOOLE

RUGBY LEAGUE LIONS

AN ILLUSTRATED HISTORY OF THE GREAT BRITAIN RUGBY LEAGUE TEAM 1907–2001

LES HOOLE

First published in Great Britain in 2001 by
The Breedon Books Publishing Company Limited
Breedon House, 3 The Parker Centre, Derby, DE21 4SZ.

This paperback edition published in Great Britain in 2015
by DB Publishing, an imprint of JMD Media Ltd

ISBN 978-1-78091-463-3

Printed and bound in the UK by Copytech (UK) Ltd Peterborough

Contents

Acknowledgements

The images in this book have been collected over many years and I thank the following who have loaned items from their collections: Tim Auty, Dave Makin, Chris Burton, Peter Benson, Mike Green, Trevor Delaney, Robert Gate, Rowland Davis and Harry Jepson. The majority of the modern photographs are the work of photographer Sig Kasatkin.

For help and encouragement I thank my wife Dianne and Ben and Verity Hoole.

The following publications were consulted for reference: *The Struggle for the Ashes*, Robert Gate; *Rothmans Rugby League Years Books 1981 to 1999*, Raymond Fletcher and David Howes; *Great Britain Rugby League Tours*, Roland Davies; *History of Rugby League* booklets produced by the Rugby League Record Keepers Club. Newspapers: *Yorkshire Post*, *Hull Daily Mail*, *Athletic News*, *Wakefield Express*, *Manchester Guardian*.

Introduction

TWELVE years after its formation, in 1895, the officials of the Northern Union were anxious that the game should spread and desperately sought some form of international competition. A stab at international fixtures had been attempted with an England XIII taking on an Other Nationalities XIII at Wigan in 1904, but the games were far from satisfactory and the spectators showed little real interest.

Then in 1907 Joe Platt, the Northern Union secretary, received a letter from Albert Henry Baskerville, a postal worker from Wellington, New Zealand, proposing that the Union accept a 26-man tour party from New Zealand to play a series of fixtures under Northern Union rules.

The Union had the vision to accept and by the end of the 1907-08 season international rugby league had arrived.

The following year the first group of Australians toured Britain and in 1910 the Northern Union sent its first tourists 12,000 miles to play the 13-a-side game in a true international context.

It was the start to a remarkable tradition that, despite the interruption of two world wars and the divisions in Australian rugby that the arrival of Super League caused, would see the best of each nations' players travel to the other side of the world to play each other at a game that is still centred around the old county boundaries of Yorkshire, Lancashire and Cumberland.

The photographs and images collected together in this book are a celebration of one of the sporting world's most outstanding success stories that, with the visit of the 19th Kangaroos tour party in 2001, continues to thrive after almost 100 years.

Tradition decrees that a British Lion plays 'Down Under', and Kiwis and Kangaroos only play in the Northern Hemisphere or whilst on tour in Australasia; however, for the purpose of this book these rules have sometimes been overlooked.

Early Days – Kiwis, Kangaroos and Lions

THE provincial game of Northern Union Football received a huge publicity and credibility boost with the 35-match tour of Great Britain by the New Zealanders in the 1907-08 season. The game could at last be seen to be expanding, and the Union's vision of playing two of the Test matches away from the heartlands was a brave attempt to spread the 13-a-side nationwide. The first Kangaroos tour, a year later, enhanced the Union further and an invitation by the fledgling Australian Rugby League to tour in 1910 was accepted.

The first Lions tour was a huge success with the game's officials transporting the tour party a total of 35,000 miles in five months of travelling. Huge crowds witnessed the games in Sydney and the tourists played their part in spreading rugby league with games in Brisbane and Newcastle.

By 1911 the Australians had become the driving force in football 'Down Under' and the second Kangaroos toured Great Britain in 1911-12 playing 35 games and defeating the British 2-1 to win the series.

In 1914, Harold Wagstaff's Lions performed miracles both on and off the field and brought the Ashes back to Britain with a momentous victory in the famous 'Rorkes Drift' Test at Sydney. Crowds for the games exceeded the ones for the 1910 tour and the Lions returned home to a £60 bonus and a war with Germany.

TEACHING THE COLONIAL IDEA.

The Tyke: "Tha's gotten t'grit an' t' physick, but tha's bahn ter dew nowt wi'aht ar bit er larnin', tha knaws."

Britain's first ever international opposion were the New Zealanders who toured during the 1907-08 season and played an incredible 32 games and three Test matches. Dubbed the 'All Golds' by the Australian press, a reference to their professionalism, the New Zealanders soon adopted the nickname 'All Blacks' after the famous strip they wore. The players were generally given a fair reception by the press but for one newspaper, which published a cartoon of the tourists in their alleged traditional wear.

Harry Wilson, the Hunslet forward who opposed the New Zealanders in all three of the Test matches against the Northern Union. The visit of the 'All Blacks' was seized upon by the Northern Union to help spread the 13-a-side game away from the traditional heartlands of Yorkshire, Lancashire and Cumbria with games against the new Welsh clubs who had entered the Union and Test matches in London and Cheltenham.

The first ever Test match between the Northern Union and New Zealand recorded by a newspaper artist. A crowd of 8,000 assembled to witness the first ever Test match between Great Britain, called the Northern Union at the time, and New Zealand at Headingley. The home side triumphed 14-6 with tries from Leytham, Llewellyn and Robinson (2) and a goal from Jolley.

Hogg of Broughton Rangers and Leytham of Wigan, the wing men for the First Test against the All Blacks at Headingley, pictured as the two players on the extreme right of the back row of this England team which met New Zealand at Wigan in January 1908. Bert Avery (the man in the hat on the back row), the Oldham forward, played 11 games on the 1910 tour including the First Test against Australia in Sydney. Avery was a highly versatile player who could adopt to most positions on the field. In the game against Metropolis and the First Test against Australia, when injuries forced changes in tactics, it was Avery dropped out of the pack to full-back. In the First Test against New Zealand at Auckland, the loose-forward scored a hat-trick of tries in the Lions 52-20 demolition of the Kiwis.

Harry Taylor, the Hull full-back who captained the Northern Union in the First Test against the 'All Blacks' at Headingley. He is shown here in the middle of the front row of the Yorkshire team which met New Zealand at Wakefield in December 1907.

The programme cover for the third Northern Union v New Zealand Test at the Athletic Ground, Cheltenham. The Union's courage at taking the game well away from the game's northern roots worked reasonably well with a crowd of around 4,000 bemused onlookers watching the match, despite the heavy rain which fell for most of the 80 minutes play. The tourists defeated the Northern Union 8-5 to clinch the first ever Test series 2-1 in an ill-tempered game

Official Programme.
COPYRIGHT: NORMAN BROTHERS, Ltd.

Price Threepence

NORTHERN UNION
v.
NEW ZEALAND

ATHLETIC GROUND,
CHELTENHAM,

SATURDAY, FEB. 15th,
1908.

A. R. BASKERVILLE (New Zealand) Promoter of Tour and Sec.

which saw the referee Mr McCutcheon of Oldham stop the game and lecture the players on their tactics several times. The travels arrangements for the two sides differed greatly; the All Blacks had travelled down on the Friday before the game, whereas the home side set off at 6.30am to arrive with around an hour and a half to spare before the kick-off. One player had actually left home at 3am and James Leytham, the Wigan centre, had been unable to get time off work, his place taken by Tyson of Oldham.

Oldham's Tyson and Broughton Rangers forward Clampitt (the two players on the extreme left of the front row) made their Great Britain debuts in the Third Test at Cheltenham in 1908. They are shown here in the Whites team for the trial match before the 1910 tour to Australasia.

Bert Jenkins, the Welsh captain for the very First Test match between Great Britain and Australia played at Park Royal, London 12 December 1908. The Northern Union were once again anxious to use the Test series as a means of spreading the game to the capital but bad planning saw a crowd of only 2,000 attend. The authorities had failed to see the counter attractions of a Chelsea v Newcastle United Association Football match and the Oxford v Cambridge rugby union match also played in London on the same afternoon. The 2,000 curious onlookers were rewarded with a superb game that ebbed and flowed, acted out with tremendous sportsmanship and finished 22 points all.

Johnny Thomas, the Wigan half-back who scored the first British try against Australia in the Test at Park Royal. Thomas continued his scoring in the second and third Tests, scoring a try at St James Park, Newcastle and Villa Park, Birmingham. Thomas was to tour Australia and New Zealand with the first Lions in 1910 making 12 appearances and continuing his scoring prowess at the games highest level with a try in all three Test matches. He played his last international game against the Australians at St James Park, Newcastle in the First Test match of the 1911-12 series ending his career with a brace of goals in the home side's 19-10 defeat.

John Willie Higson was a 22-year-old forward who had played his first football with the then junior side Featherstone Rovers. A tremendous scrummager, he played against the first Kangaroos in the first two Test matches of the 1908-09 campaign.

Frank Young signed for the Leeds club in 1906 when a disagreement with the Welsh Rugby Union left the Cardiff full-back, nicknamed 'bucket' for his ability to deal with high kicks, with a sine die suspension. He made one Test appearance against the Australians at Birmingham in 1909 and toured Australia in 1910 when his tour came to an abrupt end in only his second outing, when a twisted knee in the game against The Metropolis in Sydney tour reduced him to a mere spectator for the rest of the trip.

After much deliberation about finances the first tour to Australia and New Zealand was eventually arranged with the Northern Union's sliding scale of gate monies finally agreed to by the Australian Rugby League. The Union invited clubs to nominate players 'who will do honour to the Northern Union both on and off the field, so that the Union would have the reputation of not only having shown the best football, but of having sent out the best behaved and most gentlemanly team that has toured Australia'. Trial matches were arranged at Headingley and Central Park, Wigan and from the first selected and these games a squad of 26 players was selected to make the trip. The squad are pictured resplendent in their best suits and superb 'boaters'.

Billy Batten was the luckiest of the Lions. Picked to tour, he injured his knee and withdrew from the trip following advice from Mr Littlewood the eminent Leeds surgeon, who had informed Batten that he may never play football again. Despite this Batten tested the knee himself, found it fit for football and asked the tour officials if he could be re-instated. They agreed if he would test the injury in a match, so Batten promptly turned out for Hemsworth and scored a hat-trick of tries against Normanton St Johns and following a further consultation with the doctor was passed fit to play and travelled to Australia with the second party. The barnstorming wingman made 12 appearances on the 18-match tour including the two Tests against Australia at Sydney and Brisbane and the solitary Test against New Zealand at the Domain Cricket Ground, Auckland.

The first Lions to tour Australia and New Zealand pose for the camera, an event that would become a tradition for all future tours. Back row (left to right): Helm (Oldham), Ruddick (Broughton Rangers), Sugars (Warrington), Ramsdale (Wigan), Curzon (Salford), Leytham (Wigan), Winstanley (Wigan). Third row: Boylen (Hull), Thomas (Wigan), Kershaw (Wakefield Trinity), Smith (Hunslet), Lomas (Salford), Newbound (Wakefield Trinity), Jukes (Hunslet), Bartholmew (Huddersfield), Ward (Leeds). Seated: Dell (visitor), Webster (Leeds), Batten (Hunslet), Jenkins (Wigan), Houghton (tour manager), Clifford (tour manager), Avery (Oldham), Riley (Halifax), Davies (Huddersfield), Murray (trainer). Front: Sharrocks (Wigan), Young (Leeds), Jenkins (Ebbw Vale), Farrar (Hunslet). The Lions played 14 games in Australia, winning 10, drawing two and losing the first two games of the tour to New South Wales. They were successful in both Test matches played in Sydney and Brisbane and drew 13-13 in an international game against an Australasia XIII which comprised 11 Australians and two New Zealanders and was watched by a huge crowd of 50,000 in Sydney.

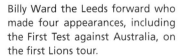

Billy Jukes, the dashing second row forward from Hunslet, made his international debut against the Australians in the First Test of the 1908 tour and went on to oppose the Kangaroos in Newcastle and Birmingham. In mid-June 1910, the 26-year-old, 13st Jukes played the game of his life in the First Test at the Agricultural Showground, Sydney. A crowd of 42,000, the largest ever for a rugby league match, witnessed Jukes cross the

Billy Ward the Leeds forward who made four appearances, including the First Test against Australia, on the first Lions tour.

line for three tries to help the Lions to their 27-20 victory and create a record for a forward that still stands today. Jukes made 12 appearances, including all three Test matches on the tour and scored 10 tries.

The Lions travelled to Australia without an official captain being announced but on arrival the managers soon appointed Salford's James Lomas. The Cumberland-born centre was one of the games first stars and had commanded a transfer fee of £100 when he left Bramley to join Salford in 1901. Although he had played against the All Blacks for an England XIII in 1908, when he scored a try and a goal, he won his first Great Britain cap in 1909 opposing the Kangaroos, as captain of the British team, in the Second Test at Newcastle. Lomas captained Great Britain again in the Villa Park Test in mid-February, when the Lions defeated Australia 6-5. On the 1910 tour Lomas was the star, scoring 136 points, from 10 tries and 53 goals, in 13 appearances. Back home his endeavours in Australia brought another record transfer fee when Oldham paid Salford £300 for his services. He made only one more international appearance when he played, badly injured for much of the match, against the Kangaroos at Villa Park on 1 January 1912.

'Gentleman' Jim Leytham topped both the try and points tables for the 1909-10 season, the Wigan wing man crossing for 48 tries and kicking 44 goals. Despite this he still had to play as a Lancashire probable in the tour trial at Central Park, Wigan in March 1910 and although his points gathering abilities left him for the game he did enough to travel with the first Lions of 1910. He played 12 games on the tour, scoring 12 tries and kicking five goals, a points total of 46 the second highest of the tour. Leytham played in all three Tests scoring two tries in the First Tests in Sydney and Auckland and four in the Brisbane Test, a scoring achievement that is still to be beaten.

Australian Jimmy Devereux toured with the first Kangaroos and later signed for Hull FC where he was one of the prime movers in bringing the Challenge Cup to the Boulevard in 1914. In June 1910 the Aussie centre became an honorary British Lion for the day when he guested, along with four other Australians, for the tourists against a Northern Districts XIII at Newcastle. The Anglo-Australian side beat the home side 24-8 and then four days later a full contingent of tourists defeated Newcastle again 40-20.

The Lions of 1914. Back row (left to right): Clampitt (Broughton Rangers), Clarke (Huddersfield), Longstaff (Huddersfield), Roman (Rochdale Hornets), Holland (Oldham), Smales (Hunslet), Jarman (Leeds). Third row: Hall (Oldham), Thomas (Wigan), Chilcott (Huddersfield), Guerin (Hunslet), Coldrick (Wigan), Johnson (Widnes), Ramsdale (Wigan), Williams (Wigan). Seated: Robinson (Rochdale Hornets), O'Gara (Widnes), Moorhouse (Huddersfield), Clifford (manager), Wagstaff (Huddersfield), Houghton (manager), Davies (Leeds), Wood (Oldham), Jenkins (Wigan). Front: Francis (Hull), Rogers (Huddersfield), Murray (trainer), Smith (Hunslet) and Prosser (Halifax). Before the Lions set sail the Northern Union were at once again at loggerheads with the Australian Rugby League about the finances of the tour and it was not until October 1913 that the expedition was finally agreed. The Northern Union would have 65 per cent of the gate receipts and the players would be paid 10s per week at sea, £1 a week on land, and £10 bonus prior to sailing.

The married men received a £1 10s allowance but the bachelors of the party had to negotiate their own terms. The tour consisted of 26 players and the party would share one third of the profits.

NORTHERN UNION NEWS

SOUVENIR
OF
AUSTRALASIAN
TOUR (1914).

HEIGHTS, WEIGHTS and BIOGRAPHIES
OF PLAYERS.

PROGRAMME OF MATCHES IN AUSTRALIA & NEW ZEALAND.

Compiled by "FORWARD," Athletic News.

Printed and Published by
E. R. SWINDELLS, 10a, Fountain St., Manchester

The tour was famous for the final Test in Sydney when pressure by the Australian Rugby League forced the Lions to play a third Test within eight days of the first. The Lions started the tour well with a 101-0 defeat of South Australia in Adelaide, suffered a setback with two defeats in Sydney and then journeyed north to Queensland and the First Test. The Queensland Rugby League had decided that they could not afford to stage the game so following three victories in Brisbane and Ipswich the party returned to play the re-arranged First Test in Sydney. The Lions defeated the Australians 23-5 at the Agricultural Ground and then two days later lost the Second Test, played for the first time at the Sydney Cricket Ground, 12-7. With the Third Test not scheduled for a further six weeks the tourists travelled up country to play Western District at Bathurst when they were contacted by the ARL who insisted the final game be brought forward and be played in Sydney by the end of the week. The tour managers protested, cables few back and forth between Sydney and the Union's headquarters in Oldham but the hosts won the day and the game was played on 4 July, only 10 days after the First Test during which time the Lions had travelled 1,400 miles by rail. Forever remembered as the 'Rorke's Drift Test' the dramatic proceedings began before the kick off at the tourist's hotel when Mr Clifford, the tour manager, made stirring speeches to the players selected to play. At the Cricket Ground the Lions lost man after man from injury but still managed to build a 14-0 lead. By mid-way through the second half they were reduced to only 11 men and then with 10 minutes remaining 10 men and for a few minutes nine men. The Australians did everything they could think of to pierce the British defence, but the Lions held firm and despite the huge task before them, hung on to a famous 14-6 victory.

The Lions of 1914 captured in their distinctive red and white hooped jerseys, the colours adopted for the first two tours of Australia and New Zealand.

Alf Francis a free-scoring wing man was brought north, from Treherbert, by Hull FC in 1910. He soon settled in his new code of football and set a new club record of 27 tries in his first season at the Boulevard. He toured with Wagstaff's Lions of 1914 but injuries restricted him to only three appearances and six tries.

Ramsdale, the Wigan forward, made his debut for Great Britain in the First Test against Australia in 1910. He made seven appearances on his first tour scoring two tries. In 1911-12 Ramsdale opposed the Kangaroos in the Test matches at Tynecastle Park, Edinburgh and Birmingham, his performances earning a second tour with Wagstaff in 1914. An ever-present in all three Australian Tests he made a total of nine appearances including the Test against New Zealand at Auckland.

A group of well-dressed tourists on a sightseeing trip during the tour in 1914.

By the 1911-12 season Huddersfield were well on their way to assembling one of the finest club sides in the history of the game, 'The Team of All the Talent' as the Fartowners were often called had at its hub Harold Wagstaff, a young three-quarter who the club had signed from Underbank, near Holmfirth. The Prince of Centres, as he was to be known, was only 15½ when he made his debut for Huddersfield and had been capped, by England, against the first Kangaroos before he was 18. He had, however, to wait until the second Kangaroos visited before he made his Great Britain Test debut against the Australians at Newcastle United's St James Park on 8 November 1911. The Lions lost that day but in mid-December Wagstaff faced the 'Roos again in Edinburgh and scored a brace of tries, his first and last in international football, to help Britain draw 11-11. On the 1914 Lions tour Wagstaff made 13 appearances, including all four Test matches and scored 11 tries and kicked four goals. He toured again as captain of the 1920 Lions and scored 10 tries in his 13 appearances. Wagstaff won his final cap for Great Britain at The Weaste, Salford, in November 1922 when tries by Hilton and Gallagher were enough to defeat the Kangaroos 6-0. He had won 12 caps for Great Britain in his decade of international football and although he contributed so much to the game he will probably be remembered most as being the captain of the British side that won the 'Rorkes Drift Test' in Sydney in 1914.

In 1906 Hunslet signed Fred Smith, a diminutive 20-year-old who was playing Association Football with Kippax, a village between Leeds and Castleford. Smith soon became a regular with the Hunslet team but was often overshadowed by the prowess of Albert Goldthorpe, his half back partner. Smith made his Test debut against the Australians in the Second Test at the Exhibition Ground, Brisbane, in early July 1910 and scored a try in the solitary Test against New Zealand at Auckland on 30 July. His appearances on the tour numbered 12 and he scored four tries. Back in England he was Britain's regular half-back for the three Test series against the Kangaroos in the 1911-12 season. Once described as 'one of the sturdiest and strongest halves in the game' Smith played for the 'whites' in the tour trial at Headingley on 4 March 1910 and impressed the selectors enough to make his second trip to Australia in 1914. He had another successful tour playing in 12 games including all four Test matches with the Kangaroos and Kiwis.

Stan Moorhouse was the 1914 tour's highest try-scorer with 19 from 10 games. He played in two Test matches, the first against Australia when he crossed for two tries and the game against the New Zealanders at Auckland where he once again grabbed a brace of touchdowns.

Johnny Rogers, the tiny Welsh half-back, who toured with the Lions of 1914 and 1920 and won a total of seven Test caps. He played in all three Test matches against the Australians on the 1920 tour but his tour was cut short when he broke his leg a week before the First Test against New Zealand. His career ended against the 1921-22 Kangaroos when he opposed Cubitt's tourists in all three Tests.

Douglas Clarke, the Cumbrian forward who made his international debut against the second Kangaroos in Edinburgh in 1911. He toured with the Lions of 1914 and collected 11 Test caps by the time of his retirement in the game New Zealand at Wellington in 1920.

The Twenties – the Tour Cycle Established

THE Lions toured Australia and New Zealand in 1920, once more captained by Harold Wagstaff, and the tour was a huge financial success despite the tourists losing the Ashes series in Australia and their first match in New Zealand. The Kangaroos made their third tour in 1921-22 and once the Ashes changed hands when the British won the rubber 2-1 with all three Test matches played in the games heartlands for the first time. Jonty Parkin's Lions of 1924 regained the Ashes in style in Australia but lost the three-Test series in New Zealand. Confident following the 2-1 defeat of Great Britain, the Kiwis toured Britain in 1926, losing all three Tests to the British on a tour more famous for the internal strife of the tourists than the matches they played. With the New Zealanders taking the place of Australia in the, by now crowded, tour calendar it was 1928, in Brisbane, when the old foes met again. Once again the Green and Golds managed a Test victory but the Lions held the Ashes with wins in Sydney and Brisbane and beat the Kiwis 2-1 with victories in Dunedin and Christchurch.

The final tour of the decade saw the Kangaroos trounce the British at Hull, lose at Leeds and, for the first and only time, draw 0-0 at Swinton. The Ashes were still held by the British but with the series drawn a deciding fourth Test was played at Rochdale where a solitary try from Leeds wing man Stanley Smith put the matter beyond doubt.

The 1920 Lions. Back row (left to right): W. Hurcombe (Wigan), E. Davies (Oldham), H. Hilton (Oldham), B. Gronow (Huddersfield), W. Cunliffe (Warrington), D. Clarke (Huddersfield), F. Gallagher (Dewsbury), A.E. Wood (Oldham). Third row: W. Reid (Widnes), C. Rees (Leeds), G.A. Skelhorne (Warrington), J. Cartwright (Leigh), H. Johnson (Widnes), J. Bowers (Rochdale Hornets), E.W. Jones (Rochdale Hornets), A. Milnes (Halifax). Second row: C. Stacey (Halifax), G. Thomas (Huddersfield), S. Foster (manager), H. Wagstaff (Huddersfield), J. Wilson (manager), J. Bacon (Leeds), S. Stockwell (Leeds). Front: J. Parkin (Wakefield Trinity), J. Rogers (Huddersfield), D. Murray (trainer), J. Doyle (Barrow), W.J. Stone (Hull). The first tour after World War One was a superb financial success with an opening crowd of 67,859 in Sydney and two attendances of 60,000 when the Lions met New South Wales in Sydney. On the pitch, however, the Ashes were lost to Australia when the hosts beat the tourists in the opening two tests in Brisbane and Sydney before the Lions gained some respect with a 23-13 Third Test victory at the Agricultural Ground, Sydney.

Well dressed and a credit to the Northern Union, the tourists arrive at the P & O Wharf, Sydney, in 1920. Back row (left to right): Cunliffe (Warrington), Cartwright (Leigh), Bacon (Leeds), Gronow (Huddersfield), Bowers (Rochdale Hornets), Hilton (Oldham), Johnson (Widnes), Rees (Leeds), Gallagher (Dewsbury), Skelhorne (Warrington), D. Clarke (Huddersfield). Sitting: Reid (Widnes), Doyle (Barrow), E. Davies (Oldham), Stacey (Halifax), Foster (joint tour manager), Wagstaff (Huddersfield), John Wilson (joint tour manager), Jones (Rochdale Hornets), Wood (Oldham), Hurcombe (Wigan). Front: Stone (Hull), Lloyd (Halifax), Parkin (Wakefield Trinity), Rogers (Huddersfield), Stockwell (Leeds), Milnes (Halifax), Thomas (Huddersfield). In an attempt

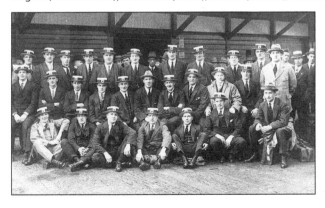

to break the monotony of the long voyage, several events were arranged for the ships passengers including a fancy dress competition which was won by Widnes forward Johnson who dressed as 'Convict 99'. The squad was to use 22 of the 26 players in Test matches and even joint tour manager John Wilson made three appearances and kicked a goal.

The Lions in action in a tour match in New Zealand in 1920. The tourists opened the tour in Auckland in late July where they lost their first ever game in New Zealand 16-24 before a record crowd of 35,000. The Lions regained their form in the two games leading up to the First Test with a 58-15 victory over Rotorua and a 49-10 win over a County District XIII at Hamilton. Another fine Auckland crowd of 30,000 witnessed the Lions defeat New Zealand 31-7 in the First Test and the tourists continued the remainder of the tour games without defeat. The final two Tests also went Britain's way with a 19-3 win at Christchurch and a narrow 11-10 victory in the Third Test at Wellington, a game attended by a disappointing crowd of 4,000.

The goal kicking points machine of the 1920 tour was Ben Gronow, the Huddersfield marksman who landed a record 65 goals in 16 games. Welshman Gronow played in two of the Tests against the Aussies, scoring the Lions solitary four points in the First Test defeat in Brisbane and one goal in the Second Test. In New Zealand he opposed the Kiwis in all three Test matches and kicked eight goals. Gronow was to return to Australia and New Zealand with the 1928 Lions but several injuries left him out of the Test team and limited him to only eight appearances.

Bill Reid the Widnes forward who toured in 1920 making 10 appearances and scoring eight tries.

Squire Stockwell, the wingman who Leeds signed from Bramley in February 1919. Stockwell toured with the Lions in 1920 and made only one appearance at Test level, making his debut against the Australians in the Third Test victory in Sydney, but in the tour games he excelled scoring 15 tries and a solitary goal in 11 games. At Headingley in 1921 he scored a remarkable try in the First Test against the Australians when with little room to work with he beat the famous Kangaroo Harold Horder to score in the corner.

The Great Britain team for the First Test against the Australians at Headingley in October 1921. Back row (left to right): Arthur Johnson (Widnes), Billy Cunliffe (Warrington), Joe Cartwright (Leigh), Edgar Morgan (Hull), Jack Price (Broughton Rangers), Jack Beames (Halifax), George Skelhorne (Warrington), Sid Foster (Halifax, team manager). Seated: Billy Stone (Hull), Gwyn Thomas (Huddersfield), Harold Wagstaff, (Huddersfield), Jim Bacon (Leeds), Squire Stockwell (Leeds). Front: Johnny Rogers (Huddersfield) and Jonathan Parkin (Wakefield Trinity). A huge crowd of 32,000 gathered to see the First Test played at Headingley since 1908 and were thrilled by a superb, close game, which Great Britain won 6-5.

A superb caricature of Billy Stone the Hull flyer who scored a try in the First Test against the Australians at Headingley in October 1921. Stone was capped eight times by Great Britain including appearances in all six Test matches on the 1920 Lions tour when he topped the try scoring with 24 tries in 17 appearances.

The 1924 Lions left England in two separate parties, the main group of 17 players and two managers left Tilbury Docks on 11 April 1924 aboard the SS *Moldavia*. Left to right: Stan Whitty, Edmund Osborne (tour business manager), Joe Thompson, Jonty Parkin, Dai Rees, Bill Burgess, Harry Dannatt (team manager), Harold Bowman, Frank Gallagher, Joe Darwell, Charlie Pollard, Ben Gronow, Jim Bacon, Charlie Carr, Frank Evans, Bill Bentham, Jack Bennett, Walter Mooney and Billy Cunliffe. The remaining nine tourists, five from Wigan and four from Oldham, stayed in England to play the Challenge Cup Final at Rochdale and travelled later.

The 1924 Lions. Back row (left to right): Hurcombe (Wigan), Knapman (Oldham), Bennett (Rochdale Hornets), Rix (Oldham), Price (Wigan), Cunliffe (Warrington), Bentham (Broughton Rangers), Brough (Oldham). Third row: Pollard (Wakefield Trinity), Thompson (Leeds), Sullivan (Wigan), Burgess (Barrow), Sloman (Oldham), Darwell (Leigh), Bowman (Hull), Gronow (Huddersfield), Gallagher (Batley). Second row: Carr (Barrow), Whitty (Hull), Osborne (manager, Warrington), Parkin (Wakefield Trinity), Dannatt (manager, Hull), Bacon (Leeds), Ring (Wigan). Front row: D. Rees (Halifax), Mooney (Leigh), Murray (trainer), Howley (Wigan), Evans (Swinton). The Lions kept hold of the Ashes with a 2-1 victory in the Tests and lost only three

other games in the tour matches. The New Zealand leg of the tour was a nightmare with defeats in the opening two Test matches in Auckland and Wellington. The tourists regained themselves for the Third Test at Dunedin trouncing the Kiwis 31-18.

Barrow's Bill Burgess and Charlie Carr, proud representatives of the 'shipbuilders' on the 1924 tour. Prop-forward Burgess played a remarkable 22 of the 27 games, scoring three tries and one goal on the tour including all six Test matches. He was to return to Australia in 1928 and when he retired from Test football in 1929 had been awarded 16 caps. Charlie Carr made seven Test appearances in his international career, which ended in triumph when he scored a hat-trick of tries in the Third Test against the New Zealanders at Headingley in January 1926. On the 1924 tour he played in 17 games including two Test matches against the Australians and the New Zealanders. He scored nine tries including one in each of the Tests at Wellington and Dunedin.

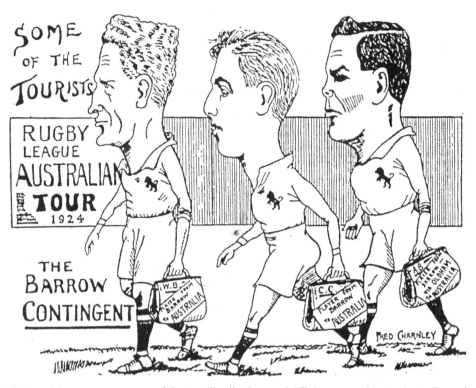

The local Barrow newspaper celebrates Charlie Carr and Bill Burgess going to Australia and remembers Albert Brough who had played for Barrow before joining Oldham.

A group of players relax during the 1924 tour standing (left to right): Dai Rees, Sid Rix, Ben Gronow, Stan Whitty and Albert Brough. Seated: Frank Gallagher, Charlie Carr, Bill Burgess and Ernie Knapman.

Frank Gallagher had an eventful first tour to Australia; in the Second Test at Sydney he helped the Lion's injury crisis when he relinquished his normal loose-forward berth to play at stand-off. In the ill-tempered Third Test at the Exhibition Ground, Brisbane Gallagher was sent off the field along with Australia's Jim Bennett.

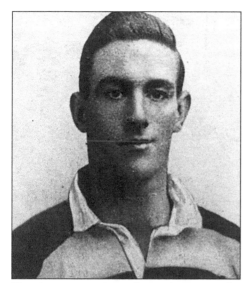

The long-gone Broughton Rangers, the Manchester-based club that were founder members of the Northern Union in 1895 supplied only three tourists to Australia and New Zealand, G. Ruddick in 1910, L. Clampitt in 1914 and W. Bentham in 1924. Wingman Bentham made seven appearances on the tour including the First and Second Test matches against the New Zealanders at Auckland and Wellington.

Harold Bowman, who signed for Hull in 1921, toured in 1924 and 1928. In his first tour he played in 14 of the 27 games, scoring eight tries. Bowman, a second-row forward, gained eight caps for international appearances, his first in the 11-13 defeat against New Zealand at Wellington in early August 1924 and his last, at prop, against the Australians at Craven Park, Hull in 1929.

A superb view of the crowd at the Australia v Great Britain, First Test at The Sydney Cricket Ground in June 1924. The famous SCG hosted 31 Anglo-Australia Test matches.

Another picture from the same Australia v Great Britain First Test at The Sydney Cricket Ground in June 1924.

Edmund Osborne, the chairman of the Rugby Football League greets Herbert 'Bert' Avery, the captain of the 1926 New Zealanders. The first tour by the Kiwis since the pioneers of 1907 was eagerly anticipated by the British clubs and supporters but was split by in-fighting and domineering management from the very start. The three Test matches were all victories for the British but the bad publicity the squabbling tourists received led to little interest and poor attendances.

The Great Britain side for the Second Test between Great Britain and New Zealand at the Boulevard, Hull. The Kiwis were no match for the British XIII who, in front of a disappointing crowd of 7,000, beat the tourists 21-3. Wallace, Fairclough, Casewell and Thomas (2) scored tries and Jim Sullivan kicked three goals. Back row (left to right): Bacon (Leeds) reserve, Smith (Bradford), Bowman (Hull), Fildes (St Helens Recs), Dannatt (Hull official), Burgess (Barrow), Thomas (Leeds), Evans (Swinton), Rix (Oldham) and Taylor (Hull) reserve. Front: Gallagher (Batley), Fairclough (St Helens), Carr (Barrow), Parkin (Wakefield Trinity), Sullivan (Wigan) and Wallace (St Helens Recs).

Arthur 'Ginger' Thomas, the Leeds second-row forward who scored a brace of tries on his debut for Great Britain in the Second Test against New Zealand at Craven Park, Hull in 1926. Thomas never toured with the Lions but won four caps, two against the Kiwis of 1926 and two for appearances against the Kangaroos in the infamous 0-0 Third Test at Swinton and the Fourth Test at Rochdale in January 1930.

One of the great features of an impending tour was the selection of the players, the rugby league press would speculate for months in advance as to who the league would pick to make, for many, the journey of their lifetime. For many years The Rugby Football League would make some automatic selections and then arrange tour trials. In February 1928 the league played the second tour trial for the fifth tour to Australia and New Zealand at the Athletic Grounds, the home of Rochdale Hornets. Such was the interest generated in the trials that a crowd of 9,000 witnessed the White XIII defeat the Red XIII 22-13 that Monday afternoon in Rochdale.

The game had a great sense of occasion with some of the finest players in the game and a host of officials. At the very back of the photograph are (left to right): John Wilson (secretary of the Rugby Football League), Tom Ashcroft of St Helens Recs and Walter Waide of Hunslet. The players are back row: Harold Bowman (Hull), Eddie Myers (York), Bill Horton (Wakefield Trinity), Billy Woods (Leigh), Arnold Bateson (Hull), Hector Crowther, (Hunslet) and Tommy Askin (Featherstone Rovers). Middle row: Oliver Dolan (St Helens Recs), Frank Bowen (St Helens Recs), Arthur Binks (Wigan), Worrall (Leigh), Jerry Laughton (Widnes) and Stan Smith (Wakefield

Trinity). The officials at the front are: R. Herbert (Rochdale Hornets), John Whittaker (Batley), John Counsell (Wigan), Charles Preston (Dewsbury) and Warrington's Edmund Osborne the 1928 joint tour manager.

The 'Whites' were victors on the day coming back from a 5-7 half-time score to defeat the 'Reds' 22-13, thanks to tries from Horton (2), Crowther and Askin, and five goals from Walter Gowers the Rochdale Hornets full-back. For the beaten 'Reds' Rix, Bowen and Evans scored tries and Bateson kicked two goals. Back row (left to right): Harold Binks, the reserve forward of Hull Kingston Rovers who substituted Harold Bowman of the Red team, Bryn Evans (Swinton), Ted Haines (Salford), Evan Williams (Leeds), Billy Williams (Salford), Emlyn Gwynne (Hull), Charlie Glossop (Wakefield Trinity) partially obscured, Tom Holliday (Oldham), Tom Flynn (Warrington), Walter Gowers (Rochdale Hornets), Joe Oliver (Batley), Jim Brough (Leeds), Albert Fildes (St Helens Recs), Charlie Carr (Barrow). The officials in front are the Mayor of Rochdale, Fred Hutchins (Oldham), Fred Kennedy (Broughton Rangers), J. Tweedale (Rochdale Hornets), J. Pennington (Wigan Highfield), A. Townend (Leeds), not known, Wilfred Gabbatt (Barrow).

The Lions pose with the crew during the long voyage to Australia.

The 1928 Lions pictured at The Sydney Cricket Ground at the start of the 24-match tour of Australia and New Zealand. Back row (left to right): Bentham (Wigan Highfield), Ellaby (St Helens), Bowman (Hull), Thompson (Leeds), Dolan (St Helens), Williams (Salford), Brough (Leeds). Third row: J. Evans (Swinton), Sloman (Oldham), Young (Bradford Northern), Fildes (St Helens), Burgess (Barrow), Horton (Wakefield Trinity), Sullivan (Wigan), Halfpenny (St Helens). Seated: Bowen (St Helens), Oliver (Batley), Frodsham (St Helens), G. Hutchins (tour manager), Parkin (Wakefield Trinity), E. Osborne (business manager), Gwynne (Hull), Gowers (Rochdale Hornets), Rosser (Leeds). Front row: B. Evans (Swinton), Fairclough (St Helens), Murray (trainer), Askin (Featherstone Rovers), Rees (Swinton). The Lions clinched the Ashes with victories over the Australians in the first two Test matches in Brisbane and Sydney. In New Zealand the tourists won the series despite losing the First Test in Auckland.

Hull's Emlyn Gwynne played 11 games on the 1928 tour including the Third Test at Sydney and the Christchurch Test against New Zealand. The Welsh wing man who had signed for Hull from Swansea in 1921 won one further cap when he opposed the 1929 Kangaroos at Craven Park, Hull.

A group of players relax during a training session at Townsville prior to the game against North Queensland in late June 1928. A crowd of 7,000 witnessed the Lions defeat North Queensland 20-2. Games in the State of Queensland have always been a great tradition of tours and many outlyling towns and communities have always supported the tourist's games well.

The 1928 tourists training at the Sydney Cricket Ground. Left to right: Gowers, Williams, Rees, Gwynne, Bryn Evans, Jack Evans, Bowman, Ellaby, Brough, Dolan, Bowen, Bentham.

Jonathon 'Jonty' Parkin captained the Lions for the second time in his third and last tour in 1928. He was capped a total of 17 times by Great Britain in a nine-year international career that began and ended with Test matches against the Australians.

MAILING LIST

LATEST DATES FOR POSTING IN THE PROVINCES TO REACH
MEMBERS OF THE TEAM AT THE PLACES SHOWN :

DATE OF POSTING.	PROBABLE DATE OF DELIVERY.	PLACE.
April 25th, 1928	April 27th, 1928	Marseille
June 20th, 1928	July 22nd, 1928	Sydney
July 12th, 1928	Aug. 13th, 1928	Auckland
Aug. 16th, 1928	Sept. 7th, 1928	Honolulu
Aug. 30th, 1928	Sept. 14th, 1928	Vancouver
Sept. 6th, 1928	Sept. 19th, 1928	Toronto
Sept. 10th, 1928	Sept. 20th, 1928	Montreal

The above posting dates have been compiled from the latest information
in the possession of Thos. Cook & Son, Ltd., and every endeavour has been
made to ensure their accuracy, but they are not guaranteed, and Thos. Cook &
Son, Ltd., cannot held themselves in any way responsible for mail posted in
accordance therewith or for any loss or inconvenience caused through non-
delivery of mail so posted.

All letters, etc., intended for members of the Team should be addressed
as follows :

Mr.
Member of British Rugby League Team,
c/o Messrs. Thos. Cook & Son, Ltd.,
Ocean Travel Dept. (Ref. OT.3D),
Berkeley Street,
Piccadilly,
London, W.1.

The back of the envelope should always bear an address to which the letter
can be returned in the event of non-delivery.

A mailing list produced for the Thos. Cook travel brochure for the 1928
Lions tour to Australia and New Zealand.

The Lions in action against Australia at Brisbane in the First Test of the 1928 series. Left to right the British players are Jim Brough, Leslie Fairclough, Bill Horton, Tom Askin with the ball about to be tackled by Aynsley of Australia and Bill Burgess. The Lions beat the Australians 15-12, taking the lead with an early Jim Sullivan goal and never losing it despite a spirited fightback by the home side. Ellaby, Fairclough and Horton scored tries and Sullivan landed three goals. Britain took to the field in their by now traditional white jerseys with a red and blue 'V' while the Aussies played for the first time in their green and gold colours.

Great Britain lost only four games on the Australian leg of the 1928 tour one to the national side, two games against New South Wales in Sydney and against Queensland at Brisbane in June. Action from the match against Queensland shows an unidentified British player tackling whilst (from left to right) Billo Rees, Joe Thompson, Bill Horton, Harold Young look on.

The Lions look bored and restless as they await the end of the ceremonies before the game against Queensland in 1928.

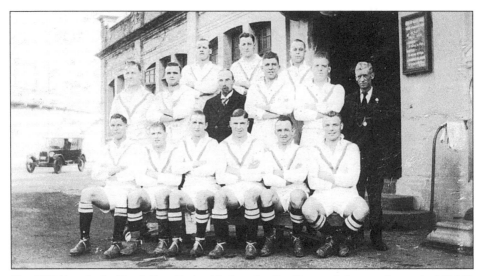

The 1928 Lions in Auckland, New Zealand before the First Test on 4 August. A crowd of 28,000 packed into Carlow Park for the game in which the Kiwis adopted a strange formation by playing with three half-backs. The plan worked because the New Zealanders defeated the Lions 17-13.

In early October 1929, at Craven Park, Hull, the Kangaroos inflicted a 31-8 defeat on a poor Great Britain side that could do little to match the tourists' speed in both thought and action. Drastic changes were made for the next Test at Headingley and one of the players drafted in to try to halt the green and gold onslaught was Arthur Atkinson, the Castleford centre. After a shaky start Atkinson's sheer strength and persistence gave him a try to help the Lions on their way to a pride restoring 9-3 victory. It was the start of a career that saw 'Brus' Atkinson play in 11 Test matches and tour Australia and New Zealand in 1932 and 1936.

Stan Smith a winger with exceptional speed and balance made his Great Britain debut in the Test against Australia at Leeds in 1929 and scored his first try in the Fourth Test at Rochdale in 1930. He toured with the 1932 Lions playing in all six Test matches and scoring a brilliant hat-trick against the Australians in the Third Test in Sydney.

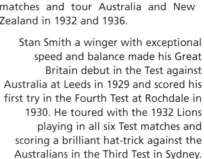

The three Test series against Australia in 1929-30 produced a win each for the Lions and Kangaroos and for the first time in the history of Anglo-Australian competition, a 0-0 draw. The Australians were still aggrieved about a last minute disallowed 'try' in the famous 0-0 Third Test at Swinton and with the rubber unsettled an unprecedented Fourth Test was played at Rochdale's Athletic Ground on Wednesday, 15 January 1930. Hector Crowther made his one and only Test appearance for Great Britain in that infamous Fourth Test at Rochdale. With minutes remaining he almost scored when chasing a kick through to the Australian line.

The Thirties – A Decade of Success

JIM Sullivan, the Wigan full-back touring for the third time, led the Lions 'Down Under' for a tour that was almost abandoned amid financial worries when the Australian pound was devalued. The fears were soon forgotten when huge crowds witnessed the Lions take the series 2-1 in Australia and sweep through New Zealand unbeaten, the players receiving a £80 share of the profits.

The Australians of 1933-34 helped promote the 13-a-side code in France when they trounced an English XIII 63-13 in Paris, but left England with the shadow of being the first Kangaroos to lose all three Tests in a series.

Jim Brough's 1936 tourists lost only three games during their 25-match tour and despite a convincing 24-8 defeat in the opening Test at the Sydney Cricket Ground, retained the Ashes with wins in Brisbane and Sydney. In New Zealand the Lions ran in 52 tries in eight straight victories to once again complete the tour unbeaten.

Australian Wally Prigg made his third Kangaroos tour in 1937 but his enthusiastic captaincy could do little to contain the British who retained the Ashes with victories in the first Test matches at Headingley and Swinton.

The tourists defeated the British in the final Test of the decade of British dominance with a 13-3 victory at Fartown, Huddersfield, in the first and only Anglo-Australian encounter to be staged there.

The 1932 Lions at the Sydney Cricket Ground at the start of the 26-match tour of Australia and New Zealand. Back row (left to right): Wright (Swinton), Feetham (Salford), Lowe (Leeds), White (Hunslet), Thompson (Leeds), Williams (Salford), Robinson (Wakefield Trinity). Third row: Silcock (Widnes), Hodgson (Swinton), Ellaby (St Helens), Horton (Wakefield Trinity), Butters (Swinton), Fender (York), Risman (Salford), Atkinson (Castleford). Seated: Fildes (St Helens), Hudson (Salford), Evans (Swinton), Anderson (manager), Sullivan (Wigan), Hutchins (manager), Pollard (Wakefield Trinity), Woods (Barrow), Dinsdale (Warrington). Front: Brogden (Huddersfield), Adams (Leeds), Davies (Halifax), Smith (Leeds). Britain held the Ashes with victories in the two Sydney Test matches and lost only two games, both in Brisbane, on the whole of the tour. The New Zealand leg, which had proved to be a stumbling block in the past, was a huge success with eight straight victories including all three Test matches.

Jim Sullivan, the tour captain, made his third visit to Australia and New Zealand in 1932 and celebrated by becoming the first player to kick over 100 goals on tour. A Welshman by birth and a Wiganer by choice full-back Sullivan had become the scourge of the Australians, his steadfast goal kicking destroying the hopes of many club and national sides. Sullivan made his debut for Great Britain in the First Test against Australian in June 1924 and within a minute of the kick-off had astounded the 50,000 crowd by giving the tourists a two-point lead with a penalty kicked from well inside his own half. It was the start of a long and memorable career during which his goal kicking proved to be the difference between the Lions and their opposition. He kicked 246 goals during his three tours 'Down Under' and would have kicked more had not an illness to his wife prevented him from making a record-breaking fourth tour with the 1936 Lions.

Alf Ellaby made his Great Britain debut in the First Test against Australia in Brisbane in June 1928 scoring a try in the Lions 15-12 victory over the Green and Golds. He appeared in 14 of the 24 tour games that year topping the try-scoring list with 20 touchdowns including four in Tests against the Australians and New Zealanders. In 1932 Ellaby was once again the leading try-scorer with 21 tries from 26 appearances. He ended his international career in the First Test against the Australians at Belle Vue, Manchester in 1933 having won 13 caps.

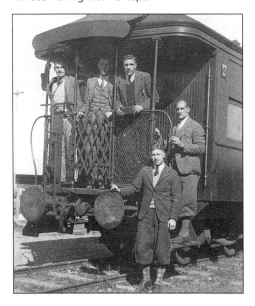

Five of the 1932 tourists board a train which was the usual method of transport for the Lions.

The British and Australian players for the First Test at Sydney in June 1932 line up with a group of officials and ex-players. The Lions are Pollard, Smith, Ellaby, Horton, Hodgson, Silcock, Sullivan, Atkinson, Thompson, White, Feetham, Brogden, Bryn Evans. Amongst the ex-players are Jimmy Devereux (third from left) and Herbert 'Dally' Messenger who were both members of the original Kangaroos of 1908. A crowd of just over 70,000 witnessed the match, which the Lions won 8-6 thanks to tries from Ellaby and Atkinson and a goal from Jim Sullivan.

COPY OF LETTER FROM MR. JOE THOMPSON
(English Rugby League Touring Team)

Hotel Doncaster,
Kensington,
30th May, 1932.

The Manager,
    Essex R. Picot, Ltd.,
        Clarence Street,
            Sydney.

Dear Sir,

I desire to thank you very sincerely for the set of "Bird" Football Studs that you forwarded to me.

I have now thoroughly tested these and I must say that they are without doubt the finest production for football boots.

The wide base prevents the jarring of the foot. They hold the ground perfectly, and the fact that they cannot bend over is a very great advantage.

The absence of nails protruding is also a very great improvement, and altogether I cannot say anything but the very best of them.

The ground on Saturday last was fearfully wet, and naturally my boots were wet through, but even with the soft sole the wide base definitely eliminated any jarring of the foot.

I congratulate you on the production, and wish you every success.

Yours faithfully,
(Signed) JOE THOMPSON.
(English Rugby League Touring Team)

Joe Thompson made his debut for Great Britain in the Second Test at Sydney in 1924 the start of an international career that brought him 12 caps in against Australia and New Zealand. In 1932 he became the first forward to make a third tour 'Down Under' and celebrated with appearances in all six Test matches against the Kangaroos and Kiwis. He also played in nine tour games and still found time to endorse 'Bird' football studs as this letter, which appeared in an Australian rugby league magazine, shows.

Leeds scrum-half Les 'Juicy' Adams played nine games on the 1932 Lions tour including the Second Test at Woollongabba, Brisbane when the Australians defeated the British 15-6.

Jim Sullivan shakes hands with a player from Ipswich before the tour match in Queensland in July 1932. The tourists defeated Ipswich 19-2 before a crowd of 3,002.

With the 1932 series poised at one Test each the third game of the rubber at the Sydney Cricket Ground was a crucial one with the Ashes waiting for the victors. Within 25 minutes of the kick-off Australia were 9-0 in front but the British were far from beaten. Three goals from an off form Jim Sullivan, a try from Huddersfield's Stan Brogden and a wonderful hat-trick of touchdowns from speedy wing man Stan Smith gave the Lions a deserved 18-13 victory and the Ashes trophy.

On 15 April 1934 a team billed as England but which contained three Welshmen including its captain Jim Sullivan met a French XIII at the Stade Buffalo, Paris for the first Anglo-French International. The British were victors 32-21 in a game that was witnessed by 20,000 curious Parisians anxious for a look at the 'game for 13' as League became known in France. Left to right: Jim Sullivan who kicked seven goals, Nat Silcock, Alec Troup, George Saddington, Joe Wright, Paddy Dalton, Albert Bailey, Alf Ellaby, Gus Risman, Bill Watson, Stan Smith, Emyln Jenkins and Bill Little.

In 1933 Great Britain became the first team to win all three Test matches of a series when they defeated the Australians at Belle Vue, Manchester, Headingley and Station Road, Swinton. All three Tests were close games and once again the boot of Jim Sullivan helped the British cause with the Welshman scoring 18 of the Lions 30 points in the three matches. His fellow countryman Les White hooked for the British in the Tests at Belle Vue and Headingley when he made his final international appearance of a career that had begun against the Aussies at the Sydney Cricket Ground in early June 1932. White had played for the brave but doomed Pontypridd Rugby League Club in their solitary league season in 1926-27 before moving North to join Hunslet where he played just short of 500 games for the South Leeds side.

The 1936 Lions attend the traditional photo call at the Sydney Cricket Ground. Back row (left to right): Brogden (Leeds), Woods (Liverpool Stanley), Davies (Wigan), Harris (Leeds), Silcock (Widnes), Risman (Salford), Ellerington (Hull). Third row: Troup (Barrow), Armitt (Swinton), Hogson (Swinton), Arkwright (Warrington), Beverley (Hunslet), Jones (Keighley), Exley (Wakefield Trinity), Hudson (Salford). Seated: Field (York), Atkinson (Castleford), Miller (Warrington), Anderson (tour manager), Brough (Leeds, tour captain), Popplewell (tour manager), Belshaw (Liverpool Stanley), Morley (Wigan), Edwards (Salford). Front: Watkins and Jenkins (Salford), McCue (Widnes), Smith (Leeds). The tourists had left North Woolwich in mid-April on the SS *Cathay*, the same vessel used to carry the successful Lions of 1928 and had arrived at Melbourne on the 25 May. A string of injuries badly disrupted the early part of the tour and the Lions lost three of their first 11 games, including the First Test against the Australians at Sydney. A win against Queensland club side Ipswich followed and the rest of the tour was played without a defeat.

Two Lions from Cumberland meet in Sydney in 1936. Douglas Clarke, the former Huddersfield rugby league international forward who toured with the Lions of 1914 and 1920 greets Jim Brough, the tour captain on the arrival of the tour party at Central Station, Sydney on the morning of 26 May. Clarke, who had won his first of 11 international caps against Australia in the Second Test at Edinburgh in 1911, was in Australia on a wrestling tour.

Jim Brough shakes hands with Dave Brown the Australian centre before a tour game in 1936. Brough was unfortunate to be a goal kicking full-back in the same era as the great Jim Sullivan, but despite the selectors' understandable preference for Sullivan, Brough did tour in 1928 and 1936. In 1928 he played 15 games including four Tests, at centre, against Australia and New Zealand and in 1936 he made a solitary Test appearance against Australia in 14 games.

Australian cartoonist Arthur Mailey celebrates the Green and Golds' 24-8 victory over the Lions in the First Test in Sydney in 1936. A crowd of 63,920 witnessed the rampant 'Roos first victory over the Lions since the Brisbane Test of June 1932.

Woods, Troup and Hodgson, three of the Lions formidable pack, line up with referee Rogers and linesman Weatherall before the Second Test against New Zealand in August 1936. Woods, a prop-forward from Liverpool Stanley made 15 appearances on the tour including five at Test level. Barrow's Troup scored four tries in his 15 appearances which included both Tests in New Zealand. Martin Hodgson of Swinton kicked 65 goals and scored three tries in his 18 appearances on the tour.

Miller, Belshaw, Field, Armitt and Brogden line up before the 23-11 Second Test victory over New Zealand at Carlow Park, Auckland. Warrington's Miller scored one of the Lions five tries.

The front and back cover of the menu for a 'welcome home luncheon' for the 1936 tourists at the Griffin Hotel in Leeds in October 1936. The rear cover has the signatures of James Lomas, Harold Wagstaff, Jonathan Parkin, Jim Sullivan and Jim Brough the captains of all the previous tours to Australia and New Zealand.

OGDEN'S CIGARETTES

S. BROGDEN (LEEDS)

Stan Brogden made his debut for Great Britain as a Huddersfield player against the Kangaroos in the Fourth Test at Rochdale in 1930, his first of 16 caps for the Lions. He toured in 1932 making 15 appearances including six at Test level and scoring 14 tries. In 1933 he opposed the Australians in two of the Test matches and in 1936, having transferred to Leeds, he embarked on his second tour to Australia and New Zealand. Brogden scored 12 tries in 15 appearances on the tour and once again played in all five Test encounters against the Kangaroos and Kiwis. In 1937 he played his final game against the Australians at Fartown, his old home ground in Huddersfield when the British were defeated 13-3.

An artist's impression of the First Test of the Anglo-Australian series of 1937. Despite being outplayed and outclassed for long periods the British scored the only try of the game through Salford's Emlyn Jenkins to win 5-4.

The Forties –
Boom Time

THE Australian Rugby League, anxious to provide Test football for a sport-hungry public, were the prime movers in the Lions tour of 1946, even lending in a hand in the booking of places on the aircraft carrier *Indomitable* for the British party.

Their eagerness to resume the touring tradition after the hardships of the war was rewarded with a hugely-successful, record-breaking series which the Lions won with two wins, a draw and a profit of £6,431. The visitors scored 783 points in 20 games including a 94-0 drubbing of Mackay, a game in which Ernest Ward kicked 17 goals.

The following year the Kiwis arrived in Britain for their first full tour since the ill-fated visit in 1926, their tour of 1939 having been disrupted by the outbreak of war. With the series locked at one Test each, a huge crowd of 42,685 gathered at Odsal for the decider, which the British won 25-9.

The international activity continued in 1948 with the visit of the Australians, the seventh Kangaroos to tour Great Britain. Great Britain retained their grip on the Ashes with victories in the opening Tests at Leeds and Swinton and with the third Test postponed due to thick fog at Bradford, the Aussies crossed the Channel for a 10-match tour of France. Back in England in late January, the Kangaroos beat the British 23-9 in the Third Test at Odsal witnessed by a crowd of 42,000.

Immediately World War Two ended, the Australian Rugby League began to press the Rugby Football League for an early resumption of Anglo-Australian tours. Although they were worried about the fitness of players from the countries involved after the struggles and hardships of the war, the British agreed and arranged tour trials at Central Park and Headingley. A squad was picked and the tour dates pencilled in before the League had thought of how to travel 'Down Under'. The Australians were so keen to host the series that the government helped book 32 berths aboard the aircraft carrier HMS *Indomitable* which was sailing from Plymouth to Freemantle in April 1946. Aboard ship the Lions were paid £1 10s a week, £2 10s a week on land and shared a third of the tour profits, a bonus of £123 per man, before sailing home. The Lions landed in Western Australia and travelled the 2,700 miles to Sydney by a troop train, a journey that lasted five days.

The Lions in Sydney. Back row (left to right): Gee (Wigan), Curran (Salford), White (York), Nicholson (Huddersfield), Bassett (Halifax), Jones (Barrow), Batten (Bradford Northern). Third row: Foster (Bradford Northern), T. Ward (Wigan), Owens (Leeds), Phillips (Oldham), Kitching (Bradford Northern), E. Ward (Bradford Northern), Murphy (Wakefield Trinity), Lewthwaite (Barrow). Seated: Ryan (Wigan), Johnson (Warrington), McCue (Widnes), Popplewell (manager), Risman (Salford), Gabbatt (manager), Whitcombe (Bradford Northern), Egan (Wigan), Hughes (Workington Town). Front: Davies (Bradford Northern), Knowelden (Barrow), Jenkins (Leeds), Horne (Barrow).

The eighth tour to Australia and New Zealand was a huge success, the 'Indomitables' as they became known were the first and only touring side to remain unbeaten in winning the Ashes in Australia. The Lions were once again plagued with injuries, Harry Murphy played only 39 minutes of the match with Canberra before dislocating his shoulder and taking no further part in the tour and Wigan's Martin Ryan was admitted to hospital for a hernia operation following an injury in the game against Newcastle. The injury situation was so critical at one stage that the tour managers cabled the League for replacements to sent out, the League replied that it was out of the question to send men with the fare being £260. Top scorers were Bradford's Ernest Ward with 101 points from 43 goals and five tries and Barrow's Jim Lewthwaite with 25 tries in 15 appearances.

OGDEN'S CIGARETTES

A. J. RISMAN (SALFORD)

Welsh centre or full-back Augustus John Risman made his Great Britain debut in the Third Test in Sydney in 1932, 14 years later and at the age of 35 the Salford captain was back to lead the Lions in his third tour. He made his final appearance for the Lions in the Ashes winning Third Test victory over the Australians at the Sydney Cricket Ground on 20 July 1946, his 17th cap for Great Britain. During his record-breaking career Risman had played in five Ashes winning series, captained the British nine times and missed only one Test, through injury.

Eric Batten was the first Lion to follow in his father's footsteps when he toured in 1946, Billy having been a member of the first Lions party in 1910. Eric, seen here attempting the famous Batten leap a tactic first tried by his father Billy in 1908, made 13 appearances on the tour scoring 18 tries. He made his international debut against the Australians in the First Test of the tour and went on to play in the final game of the series in Australia and the solitary Test against the New Zealanders when he scored a try in the Lions 8-13 defeat. His final appearance for Great Britain was in the Swinton Test against the 1947 Kiwis.

1947 saw the arrival of the first Kiwis to tour Britain since the ill-fated tourists of 1939 whose trip was cut to only two club games before the war broke out. Cartoonist Jim Forster captures the new British caps of 1947.

Wigan had five players in the team for the First Test against New Zealand at Headingley on 4 October 1947 (left to right) Ratcliffe, Bradshaw, Ward, Gee and Egan.

The cover for the First Test programme.

British captain Ted Ward touches down for a try against New Zealand in the Headingley Test of 1947 but the Wigan centre's joy was short-lived when the referee, Mr A.S. Dobson of Featherstone ruled that the pass to Ward had been forward and disallowed the try.

Belle Vue Rangers prop-forward Elwyn Gwyther scores the first British try in the First Test against the Kiwis at Headingley in 1947. The New Zealanders had disrupted the successful 1946 Lions tour with a 13-8 win at Carlow Park, Auckland and in the First Test of the 1947 series the Kiwis were ahead much of the game but thanks to further tries from Aston and Johnson, the Warrington wing man and a solitary goal from Ernest Ward Britain were 11-10 victors.

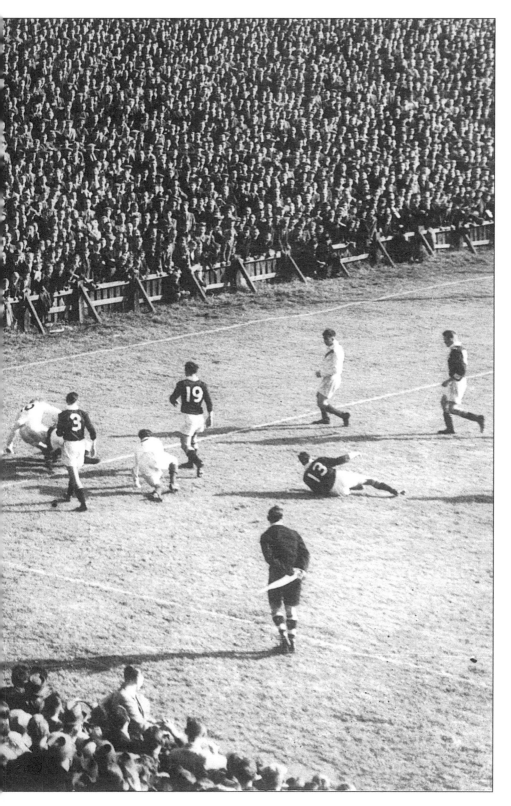

New Zealand continued their good form on the 1947 tour and, despite the home side winning the scrum count 63-16, defeated the British 10-7 in the Second Test of the series at Station Road, Swinton. A vast crowd of 42,685 filled the natural bowl of Bradford's Odsal Stadium for the third and deciding Test in late December. The British team for the game pose outside the hill top dressing rooms.

The cover for the Third Test programme.

For all the expectations the Odsal Test was a poor one, the Kiwis quickly tired and faded and the British, in superb form, ran in five tries. Robertson tackles the Bradford centre Ernest Ward, with Aston in support. Francis, the Barrow wingman, is to the left of the photograph. Ward kicked four goals, Barrow's Willie Horne landed one, Francis and Warrington's loose forward Palin scored two tries each and Ken Gee scored one.

Ken Gee the Wigan prop crashes over the New Zealand try line, in the Third Test at Odsal, for his first and only try in Test football.

The hectic tour schedule of the post-war boom in rugby league football continued with a Kangaroos tour in 1948-49. Stan McCormick, the Belle Vue Rangers wingman, swerves past the clutches of an Australian and heads for the St Michael's Lane End of the Headingley ground during the First Test of the series. Great Britain went one up with a 23-21 victory in what is often described as one of the finest of all Anglo-Australian encounters. The game was nip and tuck from the kick-off, the Kangaroos taking an early six-point lead only to be overtaken by the British and then mount a stirring last-minute effort to no avail.

With Australian full-back Clive Churchill left stranded McCormick dives for the line to score the first of his three international tries. The game was personal triumph for Stan McCormick, when he swerved, side stepped and swallow dived his way around the Headingley pitch to score two superb tries. He won three international caps, all against the 1948 Aussies and mid-way through the series left Belle Vue to join St Helens for a record £4,000 transfer fee.

The British team line up at Station Road, Swinton, for the Second Test of the 1948 series. The long-gone famous old ground had been opened in 1929 and hosted its First Test match the next year when the Lions and Kangaroos played out the one and only 0-0 draw in the history of Anglo-Australian meetings. The ground hosted 15 Tests and two World Cup matches the last ever being the 1970 Great Britain v New Zealand World Cup game.

Huddersfield's Scottish loose-forward, Dave Valentine makes a typical determined break during the Swinton Test. The game never reached the heights of the glorious spectacle of the First Test with the Kangaroos always second best to a British side that controlled almost every aspect of the game. Wigan wing Lawrenson and Warrington's Pimbett each scored a brace of tries and British captain Ernest Ward kicked two goals.

Above and previous page: Widnes-based referee Mr G.S. Phillips smiles as British captain Ernest Ward shakes hands with his Australian counterpart Billy Tyquin the Souths, Brisbane, loose forward in late January 1949. The Ashes had been won by the home nation but a crowd of 42,000, a record for a Test match in England, packed into Bradford's Odsal Stadium for the Third Test. The British front row are surrounded by the Australian full-back and five of the pack as Salford prop Curran plants the ball safely over the line for the third try of the Third Test at

Odsal. Wigan's Ken Gee hoists his hands in celebration and hooker Joe Egan moves forward to congratulate Curran. The dejected Kangaroos are (left to right) Churchill, Schubert, Tyquin, Mulligan, Gibbs and De Belin. The hosts completed a 3-0 Ashes series with a 23-9 victory over the Australians who, despite the score-line, held the initiative for long periods of the match.

Johnny Lawrenson the Wigan right-wing man who made three appearances for Great Britain in the 1948 series with Australia.

The Fifties – The World Cup Established

THE Lions began the 1950 tour with five straight victories and defeated the Australians 6-4 in the First Test in Sydney. A controversial defeat in the Brisbane Test derailed the tour considerably and Ernest Ward's men became the first Lions to lose the Ashes since Wagstaff's tourists of 1920 lost 21-8 at the Sydney Cricket Ground.

The 1951 Kiwis were beaten 3-0 and then the year later Great Britain defeated the Kangaroos of 1952 by two Tests to one to regain the Ashes. The 1954 Lions broke records galore in Australia and New Zealand but still contrived to lose grip of the Ashes once again.

In 1954 the first World Cup competition was played in France with Britain's young and inexperienced side astounding the Rugby League world with a 16-12 play-off victory over France to take the title. The crowded international fixtures continued unabated with the Kiwis touring Britain in 1955 and the Kangaroos a year later, Great Britain winning both series 2-1.

In 1957 the games against the French were finally given Test status with Britain drawing first blood with a 45-12 victory at Headingley. The Lions firm hold on the Ashes continued to the end of the decade with the 1958 tourists beating the Green and Golds 2-1 and the following year the Kangaroos winning the First Test at Swinton but losing at Leeds and Wigan.

At Grenoble in April 1959, the British lost their first-ever Test against the French, 15-24.

Four of the players selected for the 1950 Lions tour sign documents at the Rugby Football League's headquarters in Leeds. Dickie Williams the Leeds stand-off, Les Williams, the Hunslet left-wing who later withdrew from the tour to complete his exams at Carnegie College, Leeds, Ernest Ward, the Bradford Northern centre who captained the tour and Ken Traill the Bradford Northern loose-forward.

The Lions of 1950 line up for the official photograph at the Sydney Cricket Ground. Back row (left to right): Horne (Barrow), Higgins (Widnes), Danby (Salford), Hilton (Wigan), Cunliffe (Wigan), Ryan (Wigan), Pollard (Dewsbury). Third row: Naughton (Widnes), Murphy (Wakefield Trinity), Ashcroft (Wigan), Street (Dewsbury), Phillips (Belle Vue Rangers), Traill (Bradford Northern), Ratcliffe (Wigan), Osmond (Swinton). Seated: Daniels (Halifax), Ryan (Wigan), Egan (Wigan), Oldroyd (manager), Ward (Bradford Northern), Spedding (manager), Gwyther (Belle Vue Rangers), Featherstone (Warrington), Gee (Wigan). Front: Pepperell (Workington Town), Bradshaw (Wigan), Ledgard (Leigh), Williams (Leeds). A bright start to the ninth tour gave the Lions victories in their first seven games including the First Test in Sydney, but in the Second Test in Brisbane, some strange refereeing decisions that saw two of the tourists sent off for dissent gave Australia their first Test win in 13 years. A single goal from captain Ernest Ward was all that the Lions could muster against the Australians in the Third Test in Sydney, and the match and the Ashes went to Australia for the first time in 30 years.

The five Welsh players who toured in 1950. Elwyn Gwyther the Belle Vue Rangers prop, Swinton's Frank Osmond, Doug Phillips who had joined Belle Vue Rangers from Swansea Rugby Union, Arthur Daniels the Halifax right-wing who was restricted to five appearances following a broken collarbone in the game against North Coast at Kempsey and Dickie Williams the Leeds stand off who had played for Mountain Ash and Bristol Rugby Union clubs.

Programme covers from the 1950 tour games at Newcastle where the tourists won 21-10, Toowoomba, a 44-12 victory and against Queensland in Brisbane where the Lions lost 14-15.

Gordon Ratcliffe the powerful right-wing man from Wigan made his Great Britain debut against New Zealand in the Headingley Test in 1947. He toured Australia in 1950 making 11 appearances including two Tests against the Australians, and scoring six tries.

Dewsbury's Harry Street looks to pass despite being well tackled by Roy Bull in the tourist's game against New South Wales on 3 June 1950. A record crowd of 70,419 witnessed the match, which the Lions won 20-13. Loose-forward Street made 15 appearances on the 1950 tour including all three Test encounters with Australia and the First Test against New Zealand when he dropped back to play left-centre.

The British XIII for the First Test against New Zealand at Odsal in October 1951. The Kiwis were full of confidence having beaten the Lions in both Tests in 1950 but the British, out for revenge, played a fine game and were 21-15 victors. George Wilson the Workington Town wingman ran in a try hat-trick, Cracknell and Greenall each scored a try and Ken Gee kicked three goals.

THE RUGBY FOOTBALL LEAGUE

First

TEST MATCH

GREAT BRITAIN
v
NEW ZEALAND

at

ODSAL STADIUM
BRADFORD

On Saturday
October 6th, 1951

Kick-off 3 p.m.

The programme cover for the Odsal Test.

Cec Thompson, the strong running Hunslet second-row forward who later played for Workington, won two caps against the 1951 Kiwis in the Test matches at Bradford and Swinton.

Ken Gee made his Great Britain debut in the First Test of the 1946 Anglo-Australian series and went on to make a total of 17 appearances at Test level. Gee was the cornerstone of the English front row and the partnership he forged with his Wigan and Great Britain teammate, hooker Joe Egan was a huge advantage to the Lions during the late 1940s and early 1950s. Gee made his final appearance in a Great Britain shirt on 10 November 1951 in the Second Test against New Zealand at Station Road, Swinton.

The hectic international programme of the early 1950s continued unabated with a visit from the Ashes holding Kangaroos in 1952. In the face of some bitter criticism on leaving Australia the Green and Golds lost only three games on the English leg of the tour but two of these games were Test matches. In the First Test at Leeds the British beat the tourists 19-6 with Barrow's Willie Horne kicking five goals and Castle, Daniels and Ryder scoring tries. Ron Ryder the Warrington centre scores a try on his debut, and only appearance, for Great Britain much to the delight of Willie Horne.

Remembered chiefly for the acts of brutality and foul play the Third Test of the 1952-53 series is often referred to as the 'Battle of Odsal'. Britain had captured the Ashes back from the Kangaroos with a 21-5 victory in the Swinton Test and were favourites to make the series a 3-0 whitewash at Bradford, the Australians however, produced the form they had shown in the tour games and, in between the fighting, trounced the home side 27-7. Noel Pidding kicks while surrounded by Horne, Valentine, McKinney and Prescott.

Australian flanker Tom Ryan tries to evade the grasp of (left to right) Valentine, Featherstone and Dai Bevan during the Odsal Test. The match was the final international appearance of Ernest Ward the Bradford Northern centre whose 20-match international career had begun at the Sydney Cricket Ground in the First Test against Australia in 1946.

Dave Valentine watches helpless as Australian Brian Davies scores another Kangaroos try in the 'Battle of Odsal' 1952.

The British Rugby League Lions Association was formed at Belle Vue, Manchester on 18 November 1945. The Lions met at the Troutbeck Hotel, Ilkley in 1953 and posed for the camera. Back row (left to right): E. Jones, J. Wright, C. Stacey, A. Milnes, H. Beverley, T. Armitt, W.A. Williams, N. Bentham, Gwyn Davies, S. Rix, B. Hudson, and M. Hodgson. Second row: N. Silcock, W. Burgess, D. Phillips, A. Risman, A. Johnson, J.T. Woods, Bryn Evans, E. Pollard, C. Pollard, G. Rees, H. Ellerington, J. Brough, F. Williams, W. Reid. Third row: W. Crockford, W. Popplewell, J. Parkin, J. Bartholomew, H. Kershaw, J. Lomas, F. Farrar, H. Sunderland, J. Wilson. Front: F. Gallagher, T. Askin, A. Edwards, W. Watkins, J. Feetham, E. Jenkins, A. Francis, R. Pollard.

The Red team which drew 17-17 with the Whites for the first tour trial at Headingley in late February 1954. Back row: Arthur Daniels (Halifax), Frank Castle (Barrow), Lewis Jones (Leeds), Alan Prescott, Bill Bretherton, (St Helens), Nat Silcock (Wigan), Jim Bowden (Huddersfield), Phil Jackson (Barrow). Front row: Stan Kielty (Halifax), Tom Harris (Hull), Ken Traill (Bradford Northern), Jack Evans (Hunslet), Gordon Brown (Leeds).

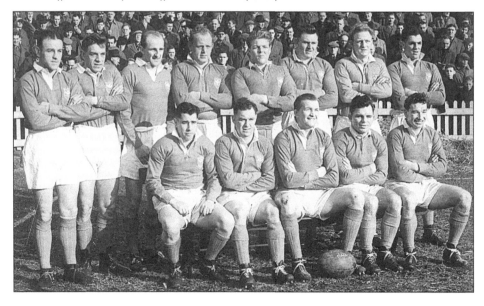

The second tour trial was held at Swinton on 10 March 1954 when the Reds defeated the Whites 20-14. The Whites team players are back row: Basil Watts (York), C. Wilcox (Rochdale Hornets), Alvin Ackerley (Halifax), Dan Naughton (Warrington), G. Parsons, (St Helens), Dave Valentine (Huddersfield). Seated: David Rose (Huddersfield), Eppie Gibson (Workington Town), Dickie Williams (Hunslet), Ted Cahill (Rochdale Hornets), Peter Norburn (Swinton). Front: Alf Burnell, Don Froggett (Rochdale Hornets).

The 1954 Lions gather for the press at the Sydney Cricket Ground. Back row (left to right): Cahill (Rochdale Hornets), Turnbull (Leeds), Boston (Wigan), Wilkinson (Halifax), Henderson (Workington Town), Cunliffe (Wigan), McKinney (Salford), Third row: O'Grady (Oldham), Bowden (Huddersfield), Traill (Bradford Northern), Silcock (Wigan), Pawsey (Leigh), Gunney (Hunslet), Briggs (Huddersfield), Prescott (St Helens). Seated: Greenall, (St Helens), Jones (Leeds), Ashcroft (Wigan), Rawson (manager), Williams (Hunslet), Hesketh (manager), Jackson (Barrow), Valentine (Huddersfield), Castle (Barrow). Front: Burnell (Hunslet), Harris (Hull), Price and Helm (Warrington). Once again the Ashes changed hands, the Australians winning the series 2-1 thanks to victories in both Sydney games. The tour and the sport of rugby league football itself was marred on 10 July in the game against New South Wales when referee Aubrey Oxford decided that enough was enough and abandoned the match, ordering both sets of players off the field after 56 minutes of mayhem masquerading as football. In his book *King of Rugger* Lewis Jones who was a spectator at the game remembers the events: 'The players simply stood in midfield, squaring up to their opposite numbers, the referee had no option but to call it a day.' Amazingly only one player was dismissed, Warrington's Ray Price and that was for swearing at the referee and touch judges.

The 1954 Lions were the first to be flown to Australia in a journey that still took four days and three nights and on the outward flight had to land at Rome because of fog. A group of Lions are pictured about to board the train for the first leg of their momentous journey.

Tour captain Dickie Williams joined Leeds for a fee of £550 in 1944 and made his Test debut in the Second Test against the Australians at Swinton in 1948. He toured in 1950 and following a club move across Leeds to Hunslet he was a surprise choice for the 1954 tour captaincy. He was capped 12 times by Great Britain and played his final match in the Second Test against New Zealand at Greymouth on 31 July 1954.

Wigan centre Ernest Ashcroft scored 11 tries in 15 games on the 1954 tour. He opposed the Australians in all three Test matches, scoring a try in the third encounter in Sydney and played in the first and third Tests in New Zealand. He had made his Great Britain debut against New Zealand in 1947 and won 11 Test caps in his career.

In 1953 Paul Barriere of the French Rugby League proposed a World Cup competition to stimulate the game at international level. The following year the four rugby league playing nations gathered in France for the first World Cup with matches played in Paris, Nantes, Marseilles, Lyon, Toulouse and Bordeaux. With the majority of the Lions who had just returned from a gruelling 32-match tour not available the British and their team of international novices were given little chance against the Australians, French and New Zealanders. Three of the British squad who played their first and only games for Great Britain were Robin Coverdale of Hull, Hunslet's hooker Sam Smith and Halifax prop John Thorley.

Welshman Lewis Jones, who had signed for Leeds only weeks earlier, bursts past an Australian defender in the Kangaroos tour match against the Loiners at Headingley in 1952. The goal-kicking expert of Rugby Union had toured Australia with the 15-a-side Lions as a teenager in 1950 and was one of the stars on the 1954 Lions tour when he amassed 278 points in 21 games. In the First Test Australian Noel Pidding set a new points in a match record when he kicked eight goals and scored a try, three weeks later Welsh full-back Lewis Jones pipped him by a point with 10 goals in the Test at Brisbane. He was capped 15 times by Great Britain scoring 147 points in his three-year career.

The Huddersfield contingent for the 1954 World Cup matched experience at the highest club and international level with a 20-year-old novice who was to become one of the Lions greatest-ever players. Harry Bradshaw and Dave Valentine flank Mick Sullivan who made his debut for the Lions in the surprise 28-13 victory over Australia at Stade Garland, Lyon on 31 October 1954. It was to be the first of a joint record of 46 caps during which time Sullivan scored a record 41 tries. Sullivan toured with the Lions in 1958, when he scored a record 38 tries, and 1962 and made his final appearance in the game against Australia in November 1963.

French wing man Contrastin is brushed aside by Dave Valentine in the 1954 World Cup play-off match at the Parc des Princes, Paris. The British defeated France 16-12 in a superb game witnessed by 30,368 to become the first winners of the World Cup.

England and Wales first opposed the French in the 1930s but it was not until 1957 that games against France were given Test match status. On 10 April 1957 the two countries met at Knowsley Road, St Helens with the British beating the French 29-14. Great Britain, back row (left to right): John Whiteley (reserve forward), Phil Jackson, Derek Turner, Sid Little, Billy Boston, Mick Sullivan, Lewis Jones, Geoff Gunney, Austin Rhodes (reserve back). Kneeling: Ray Price, Jeff Stevenson, Alan Prescott, Glyn Moses, Tommy Harris, Jack Grundy.

The British XIII who opposed the French at Grenoble on 2 March 1958 are (left to right): Tom Mitchell (manager), Bernard Ganley (Oldham), Derek Turner (Oldham), Dennis Goodwin (Barrow), Stan Owen (Leigh), Alan Davies (Oldham), Phil Jackson (Barrow), Sid Little (Oldham) and Billy Boston (Wigan). Front: Jeff Stevenson (Leeds), Mick Sullivan (Wigan), Alan Prescott (captain, St Helens), Dave Bolton (Wigan), and Tommy Harris (Hull). The British were 23-9 victors with Boston, Turner, Sullivan, Prescott and Stevenson scoring tries and Ganley kicking four goals.

The 1958 Lions. Back row (left to right): Bolton (Wigan), Carlton (St Helens), Southward (Workington Town), Sullivan (Wigan), Wookey (Workington Town), Moses (St Helens), Archer (Workington Town). Third row: Martyn (Leigh), McTigue (Wigan), Jackson (Oldham), Karalius (St Helens), Brough (coach), Challinor (Warrington), Terry (St Helens), Fraser (Warrington), Davies (Oldham). Seated: Goodwin (Barrow), Edgar (Workington Town), P. Jackson (Barrow), Manson (manager), Prescott (St Helens), Mitchell (manager), Ashton (Wigan), Whiteley (Hull), Huddart (Whitehaven). Front: Harris (Hull), Ackerley (Halifax), Murphy (St Helens), Pitchford (Oldham). The tour produced the most points ever scored 'Down Under' the Lions collectively scoring 1,196 and four players amassing over 100 points each. Mick Sullivan crossed for seven tries in the final game at Perth beating Billy Boston's 36 tries in 1954 by two to create a new record.

The Lions lost the First Test in Sydney 8-25, then travelled to Brisbane to produce an epic Test victory to match that of Wagstaff's glorious Lions of 1914. As early as the third minute the Lions were in serious trouble, Alan Prescott fell badly in a tackle and broke his right arm but seemingly oblivious to the pain the captain carried on and led his men to a brave 25-18 victory. The injuries mounted throughout the game Dave Bolton left the field after quarter of an hour and Fraser, Challinor and Karalius all needed hospital treatment when the game had ended. Two of the heroes of the Brisbane Test in action against the Australians Eric Fraser (2) and Alan Prescott.

Barrow's Phil Jackson collides with a Queensland player during the 1958 tour. Jackson played 15 games on the tour, scoring five tries and captaining the Lions in the Third Test in Sydney.

The headlines of the *Rugby Leaguer* tell the story of the First Test against Australia at Swinton in 1959. The Kangaroos defeated the British 22-14 in a superb display of football that left the home team reeling.

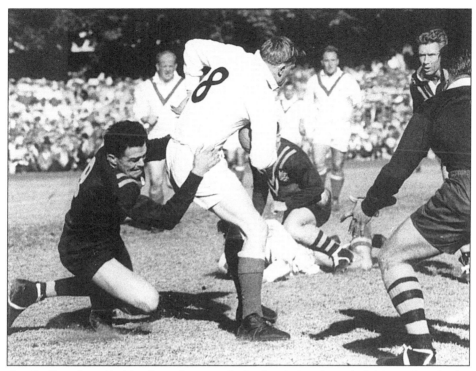

Jim Challinor is tackled by Australian captain Davies during the epic Brisbane Test. In the background are Prescott and McTigue.

The British squad for the Second Test against Australia at Headingley in 1959. Standing (left to right): Challinor (Warrington, reserve back), Fallowfield (RFL secretary), Terry (St Helens), McTigue (Wigan), Robinson (Leeds), Whiteley (Hull), N. Fox (Wakefield Trinity), Southward (Oldham) Huddart (St Helens, reserve forward). Kneeling: Vines (Wakefield Trinity), Dyson (Huddersfield), Sullivan (Wigan), Stevenson (York), Harris (Hull), Ashton (Wigan) and Bolton (Wigan).

The 1960s and '70s –
Decades of Change

GREAT Britain began the 1960s in style with a World Cup victory in 1960, a series win over New Zealand in 1961 and an Ashes-winning Lions tour to Australia in 1962. The Kangaroos interrupted the winning streak by capturing the Ashes with a 2-1 series victory in 1963 and a successful defence against the Lions of '66. The British beat the Kangaroos of 1967 in the First Test at Leeds but lost the series with defeats at London's White City and Swinton.

In 1970 the Lions regained their pride and the Ashes with a stunning 24-match tour of Australia and New Zealand. Led superbly by Frank Myler, the tourists lost only one game in Australia, the First Test, and successfully negotiated the often-difficult New Zealand leg without defeat. A home series defeat by the Kiwis in 1971 was softened with a World Cup victory in France the following year before the power in international football began to shift towards Australia. The Australian tourists of 1973 regained the Ashes with a 2-1 series win and defeated the Lions by the same score-line Down Under in 1974.

By 1978 the Kangaroos were almost unstoppable and another 2-1 defeat of Britain was followed by a humiliating Lions tour in 1979. For the first time ever, all three Tests against Australia were lost and crowds slumped to such a low that the tour was a financial disaster, the British losing £31,590. The shell-shocked British recovered for the New Zealand leg gaining a credibility boosting 2-1 win over the Kiwis.

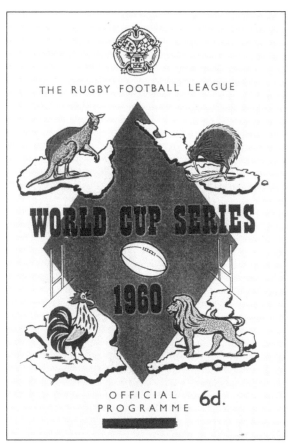

The 1960 World Cup competition was held in Great Britain during September and October with the host nation triumphing by winning all three of their games against the Australians, French and New Zealanders.

The World Cup squad training at Parkside in preparation for the 1960 World Cup.

A flashpoint in the Great Britain v France World Cup match at Swinton on 24 September 1960. The British forwards are (left to right): Brian Shaw, Johnny Whiteley, Brian McTigue and Jack Wilkinson who is being steadied by Barthe the French second row forward. The British beat the French 33-7 before a crowd of 22,923.

The Britain v France at Central Park on 17 February 1962 saw the start and finish of two international careers as Johnny Whiteley the Hull loose-forward played his last game for the British and full-back Gerry Round made his debut. Whiteley had made his debut for the Lions in the First Test against the Australians in Sydney in 1958, he went on to play four more Tests on the tour and opposed the 1959 Kangaroos twice, scoring a superb match winning try in the Second Test at Headingley when he broke from the pack and crashed over the line to give the British a single point win over the tourists.

Gerry Round made eight appearances for Great Britain and toured with the 1962 Lions and would have made far more but for a tragic car crash that killed him in the prime of his life.

The Sydney Cricket Ground in 1962 and once again the match with New South Wales developed into a rough encounter with six players, including Sayer, Sullivan and Boston, sent from the field for brawling.

First Test Sydney 1962 and the Green and Golds defence is punctured open by a typical surging run from Lions loose-forward 'Rocky' Turner. The British demoralised the Australians 31-12, their forward runners, Turner, Edgar and Huddart, cut huge gaps in the home sides defence and the Lions backs took full advantage with Round, Boston, Ashton and Sullivan all scoring tries.

Wakefield Trinity provided five of the 1962 Lions for the tour of Australia and New Zealand, Gerry Round, Jack Wilkinson, Neil Fox, Derek Turner and Harold Poynton. Prolific goal-kicker Neil Fox played in all five Test matches and was the tours top points scorer with 227 from 19 tries and 85 goals. Full-back Gerry Round, who Trinity had signed from juniors Hebden Bridge in 1959 made 20 appearances, including all five Test matches and scored 13 tries. 'Rocky' Turner missed only the Second Test in Australia and played a total of 16 games two more than Jack Wilkinson who made one Test appearance against New Zealand at Auckland. Harold Poynton made the only Test appearances of his career when he opposed the Australians twice and New Zealand once.

Billy Boston, the powerful Wigan wingman, evades a last minute airborne assault to cruise over the line for another fine try. Boston made a sensational start to his international career, selected for the 1954 Lions tour after only five first-team games for Wigan he was, at the time, the youngest-ever tourist and rewarded the faith put in him by crossing for a record 36 tries in 18 appearances. He went on to play 31 times for Britain and appeared in two World Cup campaigns in 1957 and 1960 and toured again in 1960. His final appearance came at Central Park when the British defeated France 42-4, with Billy scoring one of the eight tries the home side scored.

The British XIII for the First Test against the Kangaroos at Wembley in 1963. Back row (left to right): Paddy Armour (physio), Measures, Tembley, Bowman, Field, Tyson, Sawyer, Burgess. Front row: Bolton, Gowers, Karalius, Ashton, Murphy, Fox and Bill Fallowfield (coach-manager). In the first Anglo-Australian Test to be played under floodlights the Australians, helped by the loss of British stand-off Dave Bolton who left the field after 18 minutes, ran in five tries to win 28-2.

The programme cover for the Second Test of the 1965 Great Britain v New Zealand series. The British clinched the rubber with victories at Swinton and Odsal and a draw at Central Park.

Great Britain line up before the kick-off of the Test match against France at Perpignan on 16 January 1966. The hosts defeated the visitors 18-13 thanks mainly to the superb goal kicking of Lacaze, the Perpignan full back who landed six. Jones, Stopford and Murphy scored tries for Britain and Neil Fox kicked two goals.

Geoff Shelton, Dennis Hartley and Geoff Gunney won a total of 29 international caps between them. Geoff Gunney, a strong running and highly mobile forward made his Lions debut in the 27-7 victory over New Zealand in the First Test at Auckland in 1954 and retired against the French at Swinton in 1965. Geoff Shelton scored a brace of tries on his debut against the French at Perpignan on 8 March 1965, made 13 appearances on the Lions tour of 1966 and made his seventh and final appearance for Great Britain at Wigan in 1966. Denis Hartley won 11 caps in a career that began against France in 1964, included Tests against the Aussies and Kiwis on the 1970 Lions tour and ended in the 1970 World Cup match against Australia at Headingley in 1970.

The British XIII that defeated France 16-13 at Carcasonne in January 1967. Neil Fox (extreme left, front row) kicked two goals and Alan Hardisty (third from left, front row) and Clive Sullivan (standing second from right) both scored two tries.

Five Lions meet at the Boulevard, Hull for the Hull v Castleford league match. All five had been picked for the Great Britain v France game at Carcasonne in 1967. Left to right are Keith Hepworth and Alan Hardisty of Castleford and Hull's Mick Harrison, Arthur Keegan and Clive Sullivan.

THE RUGBY FOOTBALL LEAGUE

GREAT BRITAIN

v.

AUSTRALIA

TEST MATCH

at HEADINGLEY, LEEDS
SATURDAY 21st OCTOBER, 1967
KICK-OFF 3.0 p.m.
OFFICIAL PROGRAMME
ONE SHILLING

The programme cover for the First Test against the Kangaroos at Headingley in 1967. Britain won the game 16-11 but crashed badly in the next two games of the series and lost the Ashes they had won 'Down Under' in 1966.

The 1968 World Cup series in Australia saw five members of the Hull Kingston Rovers club picked to tour. Left to right: Peter Flanagan, Colin Hutton (assistant team manager), Chris Young, Roger Millward and Alan Burwell. The competition was a great disappointment to the Lions who lost games to Australia and France and finished in third place.

The Great Britain squad for the 1968 World Cup in Australia. Standing: Sullivan (Hull), Haigh (Wakefield Trinity), Warlow (St Helens), Watson (St Helens), French (St Helens), Clark (Leeds), Morgan (Featherstone Rovers), Shoebottom (Leeds), Ashcroft (Leigh), Young (Hull KR). Seated: Renilson (Halifax), Brooke (Wakefield Trinity), Flanagan (Hull KR), Fallowfield (team manager), Fox (Wakefield Trinity), Hutton (Hull KR, assistant manager), Millward (Hull KR), Risman (Leeds), Burwell (Hull KR). Kneeling: Bishop (St Helens) and Edwards (Castleford). Neil Fox withdrew from the tour due to injury and John Atkinson of Leeds took his place. Bev Risman was appointed captain.

The British and French sides stand for the national anthems at Toulouse on 2 February 1969. The French beat the British 13-9 to avenge the 34-10 drubbing they had received at St Helens the previous November.

The 1970 Lions were the most successful of all touring sides, losing only one game, the First Test against Australia, and drawing 17-17 with old foes New South Wales. Leeds had five members of the squad and all were rewarded with Test caps. Back row: Alan Smith missed only the first game against Australia and Syd Hynes was the tours leading try-scorer with 19 in 17 appearances. Front row: John Atkinson played in all six Tests and made most appearances on the tour with 18, Barry Seabourne opposed the New Zealanders at Auckland and Mick Shoebottom made three full Test appearances and came on as substitute in the second in Sydney.

Roger Millward was one of the outstanding performers of the 1970 Lions tour, the little stand-off scored a record equalling 20 points in the Second Test at Sydney when he scored two tries and landed seven goals out of seven attempts. It was his first of three full Lions tours to Australia and New Zealand and he also played three World Cup competitions 'Down Under' in 1968, (for England) and 1977. In total Roger 'the dodger' Millward won 29 caps and made one substitute appearance, his final game was against the 1978 Kangaroos at Headingley.

The British squad for the 1970 World Cup series in England. Despite winning all three of their games the British contrived to lose the play-off game with Australia 7-12 at Headingley.

Salford prop Coulman grounds the ball in the Second Test against New Zealand at Wheldon Road, Castleford in October 1971. The Kiwis were 17-14 victors in the game to clinch the series, the first ever by an all-New Zealand touring side. The game, which was witnessed by a pitiful 4,108, was full of incident and controversy, Britain had tries disallowed for failing to ground the ball properly and the home team were convinced Orchard had stepped into touch before crossing the line for one of the Kiwis tries.

The cover for the programme for the Third Test at Headingley in 1978. The Australians kept their grip of the Ashes with a 23-6 defeat of a Great Britain side that were almost completely outplayed from the kick-off.

Paul Charlton won 18 caps for Great Britain, his first as a Workington Town player against the New Zealanders in 1965 and his last, as a Salford player, against the Kiwis at Auckland in 1974. He made 17 appearances on the 1974 tour including all six Test matches.

The 1979 Lions squad of 30 players was the largest ever and this was boosted to 33 when replacements Topliss, Burke and Fairbairn were flown out to cover injuries. The Ashes series was lost 3-0 but the Lions gained some credibility with a 2-1 Test series victory in New Zealand.

The Modern Era

ANY lessons that could have been learned on the 1979 Lions tour were ignored and the British clung on to the belief that their traditional skills would be enough to defeat the fitter, faster and stronger Australians. The results were astonishing as the Kangaroos of 1982 swept through Britain unbeaten in all of their 15 games. The British regrouped and sent a young and inexperienced party to Australia and New Zealand in 1984 that, despite losing all six of the Test matches, displayed a new commitment and pride.

A drawn series with the 1985 Kiwis showed the British were making inroads into the gap in class but they could still not beat the Australians, losing all three Tests to the unbeaten Kangaroos of 1986. Two years later in Australia, the Ashes as a serious international competition were almost dead as the Lions lost the first two Test matches and the smallest-ever attendance of just under 16,000 turned up to witness the third game of the series. A makeshift Lions side were given no hope but astounded everyone by beating the Australians 26-12.

It was the beginning of a revival that has seen the British manufacture some superb and famous victories over the Kangaroos and Kiwis but still fail to wrest the Ashes from the grasp of the Australians. With the ending of the bitter Super League war in Australia, a return to traditional Anglo-Australian tours was about begin with the Kangaroos of 2001.

The First Test of the two match series with France in 1981 saw the Great Britain debut of diminutive Widnes scrum-half Andy Gregory, one of the finest players of the modern era. Gregory toured Australia three times in 1984, 1988 and 1992 and made a total of 25 full appearances plus one as a substitute. He made his final appearance for Great Britain in the First Test in Sydney in 1992.

British second row forward Chris Burton crashes into Craig Young, the Kangaroo prop, in the Second Test of the 1982 Australian tour. The Green and Golds were described as 'the finest sporting side to visit these shores' by one journalist as they tore their hosts apart with a breathtaking display of complete rugby league football at its best. The British were unable to cope with the speed, fitness and skills the tourists had developed and the 1982 series began a soul searching exercise that was to spread throughout the game in England.

One of the youngest and most inexperienced sides to tour Australasia were the 1984 Lions. All three Test matches against the Australians were lost but the young side played well and were far from disgraced against the powerful host nation. In New Zealand the Lions played eight games, losing all three Test matches and the tour match against Auckland. One bright spot to the tour was the first ever Test match against Papau New Guinea were the tourists defeated the Kumils 38-20 at Mount Hagen. Lee Crookes made 10 appearances on the tour.

Garry Schofield the Hull centre touches down for a try against the Australians in the First Test of the Kangaroos 1986 tour. The Australians were, once again, far too good at everything they did and the British were beaten 38-16 in front of a record crowd at a rain-soaked Old Trafford, Manchester. Britain second try was scored by Wigan's Joe Lydon who raced 70 yards to become the first British full-back to score a try in an Anglo-Australian Test match.

The British XIII for the game with France at Carcasonne on 8 February 1987. Back row (left to right): Forster, Lydon, Mike Gregory, Hobbs, Gill, Burton, Haggerty. Front: Edwards, Schofield, Kevin Beardmore, Hanley, England, Andy Gregory. The British were 20-10 victors Hanley, Gill and Beardmore scoring tries and Lydon kicking four goals.

The 1988 Lions pictured at Central Park, Wigan.

INTERNATIONAL RUGBY LEAGUE

Australian Rugby League President's XIII

Great Britain

Seiffert Oval Queanbeyan

Tuesday 5th July 1988

CURTAIN RAISER

Harold   Challenge
U15 Representative Teams

CANBERRA   RIVERINA

A programme cover and the official souvenir for the 1988 Lions tour of Papua New Guinea, Australia and New Zealand. The tour began in Papua New Guinea where the Lions defeated the national side 42-22 and a Northern Highlands Zone XIII 36-18 and then moved to Australia where the tourists won eight of their 13 games.

The Ashes were won by the hosts with victories in the First Test matches in Sydney and Brisbane before the Lions conjured up another epic win on Australian soil. The Lions entered Sydney Football ground for the Third Test with seven first-choice players missing and a makeshift fourth-choice hooker, all the ingredients for a classic Anglo-Australian encounter. Ten-nil in front at half-time the Lions repulsed the Australian fightback to end the game worthy 26-12 winners. Malcolm Reilly, the Lions coach, put the victory down to 'old fashioned bulldog spirit'. It was the first British win on Australian soil for 14 years and ended a run of 15 consecutive Kangaroo victories over Britain. Mike Gregory, the Warrington second row forward, made eight appearances for Great Britain, his finest when he scored the winning try in the Third Test at Sydney.

Hugh Waddell, a explosive running prop made his debut for Great Britain against the French at Avignon in 1988 and toured Australia with the Lions the same year. He played 10 games on the tour including the Third Test in Sydney and the First Test in New Zealand.

FRANCE V GREAT BRITAIN

HOTEL MERCURE
PALAIS DES PAPES, AVIGNON
SUNDAY 24TH JANUARY 1988

The menu card for the France v Great Britain dinner at Avignon in 1988.

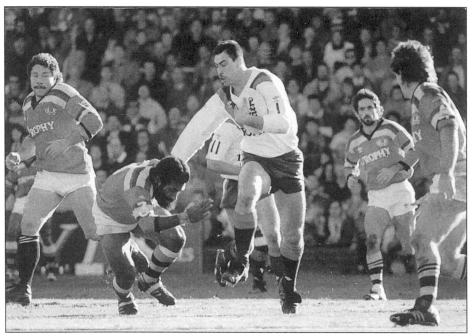

Paul Loughlin evades a tackle in the 1988 Great Britain v Rest of the World game at Headingley on 29 October 1988. The match sponsored by Whitbread Brewery was arranged to celebrate the opening of the ill-fated 'Hall of Fame' at the Bentley Arms, Woodlesford. Although billed as Great Britain, the game was not included in players' records. The British XIII held off a determined last-minute challenge from the Rest of the World to win 30-28.

Great Britain v France at Central Park, 21 January 1989, and debutant full-back Alan Tait takes the ball up towards the French line. Scotsman Tait signed for Widnes from Kelso Rugby Union Club in April 1988 and following his first cap went on to play 10 games for the Great Britain side.

Britain's front row of Keith England, Kevin Beardmore and Kelvin Skerrett prepare to confront their French counterparts in the Test at Headingley on 7 April 1990. The British Pack dominated the scrums throughout the match but the possession gained did little as the French swept to a famous 25-18 victory, their first win since a 23-13 success at Central Park in 1967.

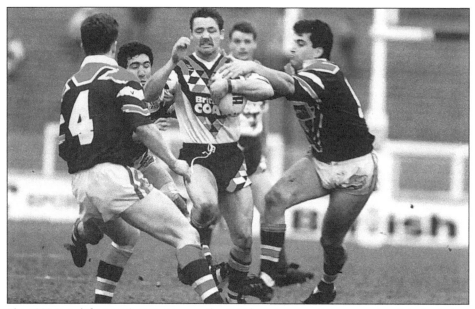

The 1990 Test defeat against France saw the British make several changes when injuries to key players gave the selectors chance to bring in new players. Castleford stand-off Graham Steadman who continued his international career with eight more full and one substitute appearance.

It takes two Kiwis to control the power of Kelvin Skerrett, the Bradford Northern prop who made his Great Britain debut against the New Zealanders in the First Test against the New Zealanders at Old Trafford in 1989. Kelvin was the nephew of Trevor Skerrett the Wakefield Trinity and Hull FC prop who won 10 caps for Great Britain.

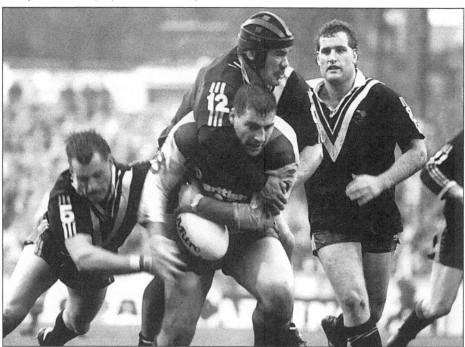

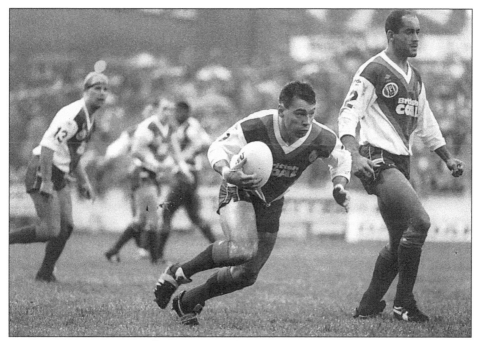

David Hulme carries the ball from dummy-half to attack the Kiwis during the 1989 Test series. The Widnes half-back played in all three Tests against the New Zealanders and toured Australia and New Zealand with his brother Paul in 1988.

The Great Britain team celebrate the victory over the Kiwis in the 1989 three-Test series in England. Wins in the Tests at Elland Road, Leeds and Central Park, Wigan gave the British their first home series success since 1965 and saw the Kiwis lose their First Test series in Britain for 24 years.

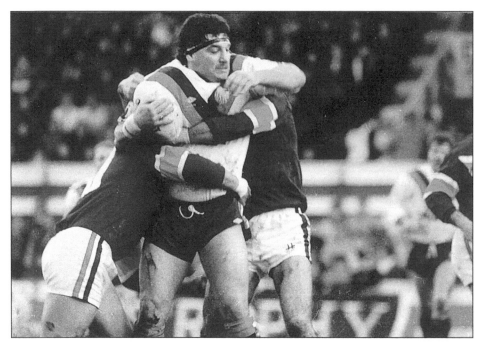

Castleford and St Helens prop Kevin Ward was one of the modern games finest forwards, a devastatingly strong runner who revelled in driving the ball up to opposing defences. Ward made 15 appearances for Great Britain and toured with the Lions of 1988.

Joe Lydon a full-back with tremendous pace won 23 full caps and made seven substitute appearances for Great Britain in an international career that began against France in 1983 and ended in the World Cup Final defeat by Australia at Wembley in 1992.

Hooker Lee Jackson evades the clutches of Mal Meninga during the Wembley Test of 1990. The British game plan of controlled style of football defeated the Kangaroos on British soil for the time in 12 years. A crowd of 54,569, a record for a Test in Britain, roared the British forward as they made a mockery of their underdog status prior to the game.

Paul Eastwood won 13 Great Britain caps but none more valuable than the one for the First Test against Australia at Wembley in 1990. The Hull wing man scorched over the Wembley turf for two superb tries and kicked three goals in the home sides 19-12 victory over the Kangaroos.

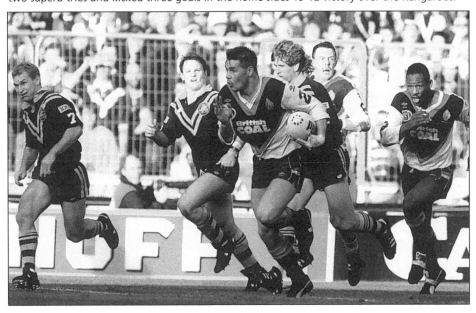

The Wigan club supplied five members of the Great Britain squad to face the 1990 Kangaroos, Andy Gregory, Shaun Edwards, Ellery Hanley, Steve Hampson and Denis Betts. Edwards had made his Great Britain debut against France in 1985 and made 32 full and four substitute appearances in an international career that ended against the Kangaroos in 1994.

British props Karl Harrison and Paul Dixon back a break from scrum-half Andy Gregory during the 1990 Wembley Test.

French Referee Alain Sablayrolles tosses the coin for British and Australian captains Ellery Hanley and Mal Meninga before the Second Test at Old Trafford in 1990. The British came within a minute of holding the Kangaroos to a 10-10 draw but a late try from Meninga gave the tourists a 14-10 victory. The 'Roos clinched the series and the Ashes a fortnight later with a 10-0 victory at Elland Road, Leeds.

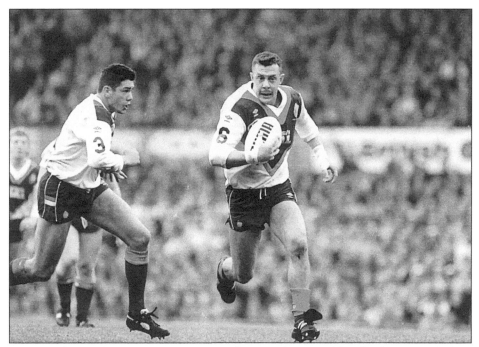

Garry Schofield and Darryl Powell in action in the Second Test at Old Trafford in 1990. Schofield made a remarkable 44 full and two substitute appearances for the Lions in a career that began against the French in 1984 and ended against the Australians in 1994.

Ellery Hanley evades the grasp of Kangaroo Paul Sironen during the Second Test at Old Trafford. Hanley won 35 caps and toured Australia and New Zealand twice, the first time in 1984 and two years later as the Lions captain.

Karl Harrison, won of the finest prop-forwards of the modern era was capped 11 times by Great Britain in a career that began against the 1990 Kangaroos and ended against the 1994 Kangaroos. He toured with the 1992 Lions, joining the tour party in mid-June as a replacement for the crop of injuries the tourists suffered.

Martin Offiah in full flight during Great Britain's 60-4 drubbing of France at Leeds in February 1991. The Widnes wingman ran in a record five tries that afternoon and by the time his 33 match career was over he had scored 26 international tries.

Jason Robinson decides where to run to avoid the attentions of two New Zealanders during the Second Test of the 1998 series against the Kiwis. The British lost the first two Tests but drew 23-23 at Vicarage Road, Watford in the final game.

Great Britain stand-off Iestyn Harris is supported by Wigan's Andrew Farrell during the Second Test against New Zealand at Reebok Stadium, Bolton on 7 November 1998.

Rugby League Football has a great feeling for its history and the players and teams of the past and every year the Lions Association meet to remember the great players, teams and games. The menu card for the British Rugby League Lions Association annual dinner held at Pembroke Halls, Walkden on 28 November 1999.

Lions Committee:

Ray French Chairman

D. Howes (Vice Chairman/Secretary)

W. Aspinall, I. Brooke,

C. Clarke, L. Crooks,

T. Foster, J. Henderson,

D. Hobbs, B. Noble,

G. Nicholls, R. Parker,

K. Roberts, A. Smith.

A Lions reunion lunch is a unique occasion for a special set of players, coaches and administrators who have represented Great Britain in the Southern Hemisphere. But it is also an event which welcomes those without whom the British Lions would not have endured for the past 89 years - the fans, the sponsors, the media, the Rugby Football League management and the referees.

The annual gathering provides for a social occasion at which all members of the league's fraternity can meet to honour Lions of the Past and the Present and further strengthen the companionship, on and off the field, which is so much a part of the 13-a-side code.

Long may it be so.

Today, the British Lions Association and the Lincoln Financial Group, sponsors to the Great Britain team and the World Cup 2000, pay a special tribute to those players who brought glory to their country by winning the World Cup Tournaments of 1954, 1960 and 1972.

I am sure they, and the British Lions present, will cherish the chance to meet old friends, re-live those magical moments of the Past, and look ahead to another century of glorious deeds on the field of play.

I hope you, our guests, do likewise. Enjoy our special day.

Ray French

Member of Lincoln Financial Group

W hat a wonderful way to introduce our sponsorship of the Rugby League World Cup next year by recognising the giants of previous World Cup clashes. It is with enormous pleasure that we are able to put right a long overdue event by presenting the Winners' medals today to the victorious Great Britain players who competed during the 1954, 1960 and 1972 World Cup Finals.

Lincoln Financial Group is proud to be associated with this great game of Rugby League - and we look forward to a World Cup next year that will project the game to its highest-ever level of popularity on the world stage.

Derek Rogers, Sales Director - Lincoln Financial Group

 BRITISH RUGBY LEAGUE LIONS ASSOCIATION

TWO

Menu

Cream of mushroom soup

Continental Bread with Butter

Poached supreme of Chicken with a Forestire Sauce

Seasonal Vegetables & Potatoes

Dutch Apple Flan served with Fresh Cream

Cheese Plate with Butter & Crackers

Fresh Ground Coffee with Mints

THREE

ND - #0217 - 270225 - C0 - 234/156/7 - PB - 9781780914633 - Gloss Lamination